Contemplations On
The Amritanubhava of
Shri Jnaneshwar Maharaj

By Sadguru Kedarji

The Bhakta School of Transformation, Inc.
Youngstown, Ohio

Contemplations On
The Amritanubhava of
Shri Jnaneshwar Maharaj

By Sadguru Kedarji

Copies of this book may be ordered through booksellers or by contacting:

The Bhakta School of Transformation, Inc.
330-623-7388 Ext 10

NityanandaShaktipatYoga.org

ISBN: 979-8-218-23257-3

Printed in the United States of America

Contents

Introduction   v
Who Is Shri Jnaneshwar Maharaj?   vii
About Sadguru Kedarji   x
Prayer to Shri Jnaneshwar Maharaj   xiv
How to Use the Contemplations   xv

Chapter 1
The Shiva-Shakti Power   1

Chapter 2
Praise for the Sadguru   13

Chapter 3
The Debt of Speech Per Se   27

Chapter 4
The Destruction of
Ignorance By Knowledge   33

Chapter 5
Existence, Knowledge and Bliss   40

Chapter 6
Disproving the Word   51

Chapter 7
Ignorance Is Imaginary   68

Chapter 8
Knowledge Per Se   114

Chapter 9
The State of Liberation Defined   118

Introduction

Acknowledgement is offered to Ramchandra Keshav Bhagwat whose translation of the Amritanubhava from Marathi has inspired this work.

My Shri Gurudev, Muktananda Paramahamsa offered many lessons from the wisdom utterances of Jnaneshwar Maharaj whom he considered to be one of the greatest Siddhas to have ever graced this planet. I owe my understanding of Shri Jnaneshwar's instruction and wisdom to my Guru who was a master at elucidating the utterances of Jnanadeva in a way that made application of Jnanadeva's wisdom to daily experience an easy reality.

The Amritanubhava is a complete embodiment of Joy in Daily Living. This is the true meaning of the Mantra Amritanubhava – *Joy In Daily Living.* There is a state to be experienced beyond the mind and beyond the senses. This state we call Witness Consciousness. There is an indweller, a witness to your mind, also known as the Observer. This Observer is a spiritual, witnessing awareness that is always present. This Witness or Observer is who you really are.

Shri Jnaneshwar Maharaj, also known as Jnanadeva, was a great Siddha Guru who knew and taught the importance of employing one's spiritual witnessing awareness in everyday existence, in order to have an ongoing experience of Joy in daily living. That is the focus of this work – to provide the wisdom necessary for reining in the restless mind in order to experience Joy.

In this regard, Jnanadeva emphasizes the importance of understanding Maya, the illusory aspect of this world-appearance, and how this Maya gives rise to an imaginary ignorance that is borne of the bondage of words. This bondage is embodied in what is known as Matrika Shakti or Matruka – the un-understood mother of the

Universe of all the worlds.

In beautifully poetic fashion, Jnaneshwar Maharaj leads us through the intricacies of the Matrika and how to gain release from the prison of words. To Jnanadeva it is incredibly important for us to attain that state that is beyond words, beyond thinking and beyond the senses, so that Joy becomes a constant in our lives. He is resolute in conveying that duality is imaginary and that contact with people, places and things should only serve to increase our experience of Bliss.

"In the court-yard of duality, the Self, the Shakti of the Supreme, of its own accord, threads through everything. When this fact is realized and experienced from moment to moment, as duality and differences appear to widen, the inner experience of unity becomes stronger. In this state, the enjoyment of sense objects only reinforces the experience of the highest Bliss, as one is reminded, over and over again, that sensory enjoyment belongs to the Universal Experient, the only doer, the only Cause – that all these are Divine expressions of that Universal Experient."

~ Jnaneshwar Maharaj, from his Amritanubhava

After explaining why ignorance is imaginary, thereby rendering knowledge as only an educational term for what is, always has been and always will be, Jnanadeva then completes his instruction by defining and sharing experiences of the state of Liberation. He clearly indicates that, with the Grace and Blessings of a Sadguru, it is entirely possible to live in a state of Grace. Combined with the Grace of our own self-effort, an intoxication of Joy can be our steady, uninterrupted experience, as we merge with the Witness to the mind – dwelling forever in a state of Bliss that is beyond the mind and beyond the senses.

Who Is
Shri Jnaneshwar Maharaj?

The name Jnaneshwar means Lord of Wisdom.
Jnanadeva, as he is also called, was one of the greatest
Siddhas in my Siddha lineage. My Guru, Muktananda
Paramahamsa, considered Jnaneshwar to be one of the
greatest sages of all the worlds. Gurudev spoke of
Jnanadeva often and taught many lessons from
Jnaneshwar's sacred texts.

Shri Jnaneshwar Maharaj was born in the small
town of Apegaon near Paithan, on the banks of the river
Godavari, in Maharashtra, India on the 15th of August,
1275. He took live Mahasamadhi, willfully dropping his
body on the 25th of November, 1296 in Alandi. Though he
lived for only 21 years he had an impact on millions of
people around the globe. His writings are considered to be
the centerpiece of scriptural study and his wisdom is the
subject of the most auspicious instruction for Sadhana. His
brother, Nivritthi, was his Guru.

At the age of 16 he wrote the *Jnaneshwari* (also
known as the *Bhavarthadipika*), a commentary on the
Bhagvad Gita of Shri Krishna. In doing so, Jnaneshwar
brought this knowledge to the common person who was not
of the Brahmin caste and did not, otherwise, have access to
such sacred texts.

A year later he wrote the *Amritanubhava* on which
these contemplations are based. He also wrote
Changadeva Pasasthi that is a letter to the famous yogi
Changadeva in which he speaks about what Self-realization
is and how it is possible to attain Liberation in this very
life. Jnaneshwar also wrote many songs known as
abhangas, such as the *Haripatha* and *Pasadayan*.
Abhangas are spiritual, devotional songs in the Marathi
language.

His father, Vitthalpant, had taken sannyasa (vows of monkhood) while still married to his mother, Rakhumabai. Vitthalpant left his wife without telling her that he intended to take sannyasa and live in his Guru's ashram, never to return home. He snuck off to live in Varanasi with his Guru, Ramanand Swami. However when his Guru found out that he had a wife, he sent Vitthalpant home to fulfill his duty to his wife and to have children.

Their first child, a pure, calm and quiet son, was named Nivritthi that means to turn inward to go beyond the mind and the senses. The second born child was Jnaneshwar. The third was Muktabai and the last was a boy, Sopanadeva. Vitthalpant was a Brahmin but because he had taken sannyasa and then left his Guru's ashram while relinquishing the vows of a monk, he was proclaimed an outcast of the Brahmin caste and could no longer perform his duties as a Brahmin priest. He and his family were forced to move to the outskirts of the village to live. They were shamed as those who defile Brahmins.

Because of this Vitthalpant was not able to find work to support his family and the shopkeepers in the village would not sell goods or food to him. The Brahmin elders told Vitthalpant that the only way to cure his sin against the Brahmin caste was to commit suicide. Horrified and depressed, Vitthalpant threw himself in a nearby river and drowned. His wife followed suit by ending her own life. The children now had to care for themselves.

They travelled to Nasik to get letters of certification that they were of the Brahmin caste so that they could go to school and get work in the region. But everywhere they went, news of Vitthalpant had preceded them and they were denied verification that they had been born as Brahmins. This made their lives exceedingly difficult.

Outside Nasik, in the holy town of Trimbakeshwar, Nivritthi found his guru, Gahininath, a follower of the Natha tradition. With the initiation and leadership of Gahininath, Nivritti became Nivrittinatha, the Guru to his brother, Jnaneshwar Maharaj.

Although Jnaneshwar was initiated into the Natha

tradition, he taught Bhakti Yoga, the path of Devotion. Jnanadeva formed a strong friendship with the poet saint, Namadeva. Together with his sister Muktabai and brother, Sopanadeva, the four travelled through India offering song sermons that became legendary. Jnaneshwar would give talks on Bhakti and the importance of Mumukshutva (the burning longing to be free). Namadeva would recite spiritual poetry. Sopanadeva would sing the poems and lead people in chanting, and Muktabai gave Shaktipat (full Kundalini awakening). In places like Pandhapur these song sermons would go on for many hours and the chanting turned into people dancing in the streets while singing the name of God.

Shri Jnaneshwar Maharaj was considered to be a Janma Siddha, born God-realized. His offering to the world continues to rescue millions from the ignorance of worldliness.

About Sadguru Kedarji

Sadguru Kedarji is the Founder of The Bhakta School of Transformation, an Ohio-based not-for-profit public charity devoted to lasting Inner Peace and permanent spiritual transformation. The curriculum offering here is based on Kedaji's *4 Pillars of Joy In Daily Living*.

He had an early career in the Performing Arts as an actor and singer in Broadway musicals, plays, movies and television. He went on to study violin and conducting at the Juilliard School of Music and graduated with degrees in performance and composition from the Manhattan School of Music. Later, he studied Eastern and Oriental Medicine, graduated with degrees in both from the Kushi Institute, and had a practice in New York City for many years.

Leading With Love

Sadguru Kedarji helps people embrace the Grace in life's joys and challenges in a way that causes lasting happiness and peace. In a world seemingly mad with greed and corruption, Kedarji has a long track record of helping people affirm and expand the best parts of their lives.

He is a Sadhu in the lineage of the great sage and saint, Bhagawan Nityananda of Ganeshpuri. He imparts the same instruction and leadership he was taught— the same methods used by a line of spiritually proven and powerful masters who have uplifted people's lives for thousands of years.

A Sadhu is one who has made the commitment to live as an ascetic, renouncing the pursuit of worldly pleasures and fantasies to serve the greater good and to work to uplift humanity. In this regard, Kedarji is also known as a Sadguru, meaning true spiritual leader, and a Shaktipat Guru (see below) who leads by example in becoming both wise and well with a powerful, heart-centered approach.

Practical Leadership
In A Shaktipat Guru

Kedarji has a reputation for leading without insisting that people follow. This allows students and seekers to come to our approach in their own way. Although 'Sadguru' is an affectionate term used by those who have benefited from his leadership, for Kedarji, the reference to Sadguru is a reference to our lineage of Sadgurus on whose shoulders he stands and takes refuge in. This is the great Shiva lineage that Bhagawan Nityananda of Ganeshpuri also made, of which Kedarji is a part.

Wise, Happy and Well

Many of Kedarji's students say that, through his leadership, he has transformed their lives in profound ways not experienced in other modalities or on other paths.

His students blossom and uncover hidden strengths through a well-integrated and time-tested approach. Through his leadership, it's possible for anyone and everyone to experience life's magic in a way that they come to know their true nature and attain a state of lasting happiness, peace and joy.

With his 4 Pillars of Joy In Daily Living as the foundation (the Spiritual Power, Improved Mental State, Emotional Resilience and Vibrant Health), he combines the power of Grace of his spiritual lineage with the time-honored, Siddha Science of the Yoga of the Siddhas. This powerful combination includes his skill as a Shaktipat Meditation master.

Authentic Shaktipat Guru – Shaktipat Meditation Master

Sadguru Kedarji is a Shaktipat Guru. He has been vested with the power and authority to fully awaken and nurture the dormant spiritual awareness known as Kundalini. Specifically, this awakening occurs by way of the transmission of the Grace-bestowing power inherent in the Blessing of Shaktipat. In particular, you will find that Sadguru Kedarji is a recognized and very skilled spiritual leader and Shaktipat Meditation Master. Additionally, his is the ability to lead you on the journey to the realization of your true nature or Self-Realization. Indeed, this is a journey in which you retrace your steps back to God.

Author/Producer

Sadguru Kedarji is the author of several books and courses, including:

- Vibration of Divine Consciousness. A Spiritual Autobiography.
- The Verses On Witness Consciousness.
- The Abode of Grace - Bhagawan Nityananda of Ganeshpuri.
- How To Be Fearless, Happy and Resilient In The Age of Noise and Distractions (a video home-study course and weekend retreat).
- The Sutras On The 5-Fold Act of Divine Consciousness.
- Live Strong and Be Happy. Learn The Daily Rituals of The Most Spiritually-Powerful, Happiest and Healthiest People On The Planet.

Spiritual Journey

Sadguru Kedarji began his quest to understand and fully imbibe Yoga Science at an early age. Feeling incomplete, Kedarji began an intense spiritual journey that took him to India and Asia. Soon after, he experienced an initiation, an awakening into the power of true Meditation, Chanting and Contemplation that formed the foundation for putting all the pieces together.

Due to this event and ongoing application of the methods taught connected to it, Kedarji was able to fully apply the science behind well-being that is based on the Spiritual Power. He calls it the energy substratum of everything. His direct, unfolding experience of this power is the basis for the integration of his 4 Pillars of Joy In Daily Living embodied in his unique approach: An approach that combines Siddha Science and the science of a holistic lifestyle of health and well-being with the transmission of Grace that he extends as a God-realized, Shaktipat Guru.

Prayer to
Shri Jnaneshwar Maharaj

Salutations to Shri Jnaneshwar Maharaj, the Doyen of
Samkhya Yoga – Disciple of Nivrittinatha and beloved of
Sopanadeva, Muktabai and Namadeva.

Son and beloved of Vitthalpant and Rakhumabai, lover of
Shri Krishna and beloved of Shri Krishna – to that
Jnanadeva I bow.

Pillar of Bhakti, author of the Bhavarthadipika and
Amritanubhava, son of Dharma and King of Gurus – to that
Jnanadeva I bow.

Beloved of Muktananda Paramahamsa, worshipped by
Siddhas, Master of the Vedas, Mad Lover of God – to that
Jnanadeva I bow.

May this offering please you and move you to grant your
Grace and Blessings to all who read these pages.

Om Shri Gurudev Jnaneshwar Maharaj Om

How to Use the Contemplations

In this book, the words "the Supreme," "the Atman," "the Self," "Consciousness" and "God" are used interchangeably and are all references to the formless Absolute, the One God.

These contemplations have manifested out of many years of offering lessons on the Amritanubhava in programs and courses. Each is designed to be contemplated and not just merely to be read.

To contemplate means to steadily regard with your heart, without prejudging or forming premature notions about that which you are contemplating. It is best to perform each contemplation inwardly in silence for approximately 3-4 minutes. While performing a contemplation, observe what you experience inside, along with the state of your mind and any inner shifts in your awareness and inner state.

It is best to record in a journal whatever you experience and observe as you perform each contemplation. A specific contemplation can be performed more than once. The contemplations do not have to be performed in any particular sequence or order and you can start wherever you like.

Journaling your observations and inner experiences is very useful.

Chapter 1
The Shiva-Shakti Power

Contemplation 1

I bow to and cherish the Shiva-Shakti power, borne of the
union of Shiva and Shakti from whom the Universe of all
the worlds manifests, is sustained and then withdrawn.

Contemplation 2

That Shiva who is the personification of Love desires to
experience this Supreme Love. Out of this desire, Shiva
becomes the beloved Shakti in order to reflect Shiva's Joy
as the manifestation of this world-appearance to enjoy
himself.

Contemplation 3

Shiva and Shakti are One being, the formless Absolute. Out
of Love the Shiva-Shakti power manifests this world-
appearance that reflects duality when Supreme,
unconditional Love is forgotten.

Contemplation 4

Shiva and Shakti appear to be different when they are
actually One. However, their being One is also imaginary
from the perspective of the material world, meaning their
Oneness cannot be properly understood from the duality of
worldliness.

Contemplation 5

Shiva and Shakti sustain an intense desire to enjoy each other by way of manifesting the appearance of duality and diversity, while never allowing any break in their unity.

Contemplation 6

Desiring to experience their existence in form to display their unity, they manifested a child known as the Universe of all the worlds. Although giving the appearance of duality in this way, their Love remained unbroken.

Contemplation 7

Engaged in the manifestation, sustenance and withdrawal of all sentient and insentient beings and things, Shiva and Shakti are never influenced in the least by this activity.

Contemplation 8

They embody the same authority and power and are filled with the same Light of Consciousness. In this way, they exist in a state of delight throughout eternity.

Contemplation 9

Being referred to as Shiva and Shakti for the sake of distinction they attempted to find duality and diversity amidst their distinction. Finding it impossible to prove such a distinction, the lost themselves in the Bliss of their undying union.

Contemplation 10

Shakti has become perfect through Paramshiva (the formless Absolute), while that Paramshiva is not perceived except by the play of the Shakti.

Contemplation 11

Their Love for each other is Supreme. Finding the Universe too small to dwell in, they delight in becoming even the tiniest particle, everywhere.

Contemplation 12

They are called the Shiva-Shakti Power because, without abiding in each other, they manifest nothing. Abiding in each other, they are the life force of the Universe of all the worlds.

Contemplation 13

In the entire Universe of all the worlds, only Shiva and Shakti (the transcendental and the immanent) exist. When the Master of the Universe sleeps, the Shakti remains immanent in all forms playing all the roles.

Contemplation 14

When awareness of the Shiva-Shakti Power is elevated the Universe of all the worlds is devoured in the indescribable Joy of the Self. Then the realization comes that God alone exists.

Contemplation 15

Shiva and Shakti are not two. They are *That* – the Self. They appear to become two for the sake of carrying out the play of the Shakti as this world. In this way, the Self is the great actor – the only Player.

Contemplation 16

Shiva exists as the Supreme Subject, and Shakti the object of Shiva's enjoyment. They live as the embodiment of Bliss due to this union.

Contemplation 17

God alone exists as both the formless Absolute and the world of forms. Any distinction as to Shiva and Shakti being male and female is a matter of impure understanding. Shiva and Shakti are One and the Universe of all the worlds manifests, is sustained and withdrawn by the Shiva-Shakti Power.

Contemplation 18

Just as separate flowers of the same plant produce only one fragrance and two lamps produce the same light, Shiva and Shakti are that One God.

Contemplation 19

The perception of Shiva and Shakti being separate beings is like believing that one can talk with one lip. Two lips are required to talk, even though they are part of the same, one body. Shiva and Shakti are the one body of Divine Consciousness that pervades the Universe of all the worlds.

Contemplation 20

Just as an intimate couple can enjoy the very same dish, Shiva and Shakti appear to be a couple for the sake of existing in eternity deriving Joy from their play.

Contemplation 21

Just as a chaste and devoted wife cannot subsist without her husband, Shakti cannot exist without Shiva. And, without Shakti, the Universal Experient and only doer, Shiva cannot be perceived and experienced.

Contemplation 22

Shakti's existence allows Shiva to be perceived and experienced as the Universal Experient, the One God. In this way, they cannot be separated or known as being different from one another.

Contemplation 23

Just as sugar is one with its sweetness and camphor is one with its fragrance, any attempt to understand and experience distinction between sugar and sweetness and camphor and fragrance is nullified. In the same way, any attempt to make a distinction between Shiva and Shakti is useless.

Contemplation 24

Can one perceive the light given off by fire without the flame that creates it? So, when contemplating the state of Shakti, only Shiva is attained.

Contemplation 25

No separation can be made between the Sun and its rays. The light of the Sun is the Sun only, and yet when the distinction between the Sun and its rays dissolves, the light of the Sun is what remains.

Contemplation 26

There can be no reflection of an object without that which is being reflected. Therefore, that which is being reflected, the Supreme Subject or formless Absolute parades itself as duality when, in fact, duality is imaginary and only the Supreme Subject exists.

Contemplation 27

Shakti exists in union with that which is formless. How then can it be said that Shakti has formed union with a person? It is due to Paramshiva's will (the will of the formless Absolute) that Shakti has become prominent.

Contemplation 28

Shiva cannot be perceived without Shakti and Shiva is the possessor of Shakti.

Contemplation 29

By the will of the Shakti, the Universe of all the worlds manifests, is sustained and withdrawn. This is how Shakti glorifies Shiva.

Contemplation 30

Shiva has no form and can only be perceived by Shakti's power. Shakti dresses Shiva up with all the forms and names of the Universe of all the worlds.

Contemplation 31

Being so fortunate, Shakti puts on a grand play with the multitude of forms to make Shiva appear diverse.

Contemplation 32

Shakti honors Shiva and Shiva honors Shakti. In this way, the fame and glory of one is hidden in the honor and existence of the other.

Contemplation 33

Out of intense desire to experience Shakti, Shiva
recognizes Shakti's existence only. Upon failing to
recognize Shakti, Shiva disappears.

Contemplation 34

By way of embracing his Shakti, Shiva manifests the
Universe of all the worlds. Without Shakti, Shiva cannot
be perceived.

Contemplation 35

Shiva loses himself in the expansion of Shakti and remains
in subtle form. Shiva possesses the Universe of all the
worlds by Shakti's Grace.

Contemplation 36

Shakti manifests Shiva's presence by way of causing
objects (people, places and things) to manifest in
Consciousness. Shiva devours these, along with Shakti,
and dissolves these objects in his formlessness.

Contemplation 37

Shakti gives birth to the Universe of all the worlds to
glorify Shiva. When Shakti takes rest, these worlds
dissolve in Paramshiva, the formless Absolute.

Contemplation 38

Shiva remains formless without Shakti and Shakti does not
exist without Shiva. In this way, the two are perfect
mirrors of each other.

Contemplation 39

Without Shakti, Shiva cannot enjoy the Bliss of the Self.

Contemplation 40

Shakti embodies Shiva. Shiva is the lover and beauty of Shakti. Together they express the world of forms in their own ecstasy.

Contemplation 41

Just as wind cannot be separated from motion and gold cannot be separated from its luster, Shiva and Shakti are inseparable and form one whole.

Contemplation 42

Where there is heat, there is fire. Where there is fragrance, there is musk. In the same way, where there is Shakti, there is Shiva. Shakti belongs to Shiva alone.

Contemplation 43

At the end of the gloaming (as the Sun has just set), night has not yet begun and day has ceased. Similarly, upon close observation of Shiva and Shakti, there is a point at which all perceived duality dissolves and there is no distinction between world and God.

Contemplation 44

In the union of Shiva and Shakti the Mantra Om is experienced in the manifestation, sustenance and withdrawal of the Universe of all the worlds. This is experienced in the space between the breaths.

Contemplation 45

Shiva and Shakti, having devoured the sweet dish of names and forms, display the true meaning of their Oneness. To that Shiva-Shakti power Jnanadeva says, "I bow."

Contemplation 46

In their mutual embrace, Shiva and Shakti dissolve in the formless Absolute, transforming ignorance into pure knowledge.

Contemplation 47

Attempting to determine their true nature by way of gross speech is futile. Shiva and Shakti are realized in the merging of the mind in silence, just as a river disappears in the ocean and is no longer a river.

Contemplation 48

No matter how powerful, the wind is always absorbed in the sky. And the brilliance of the Sun is swallowed up by clouds.

Contemplation 49
In this way, when observing the Shiva-Shakti Power closely, the seer and the act of seeing dissolve. To such and omniscient power, I bow over and over again.

Contemplation 50

Immersion in the Shiva-Shakti Power is sometimes referred to as Knowledge. However, when one is immersed in that power, everything and everyone disappears. Then there is neither knowledge or ignorance.

Contemplation 51

Even the distinction of bowing to Shiva and Shakti implies a separation from them in my bowing to them. Such a separation does not exist and my bowing is a play of the Shakti.

Contemplation 52

Just as the gold ornament is not separate and distinct from the gold from which it is made, my bowing is Shiva bowing to Shiva and Shakti bowing to Shakti.

Contemplation 53

In pronouncing the word 'speech,' it appears that the one pronouncing the word is separate from the word being pronounced. Yet the word 'speech' is one with the pronouncer of the word. There is no distinction whatsoever. (Note: In this Yoga science, the knower, that which is to be known and the means of knowing are all one in the same.)

Contemplation 54

When a river meets and merges in the ocean, is there really any distinction in their water?

Contemplation 55

The Sun and the means by which the Sun illuminates an object are one in the same. There is no difference between the Sun, its light and the means by which the Sun casts its light.

Contemplation 56

The light of the moon is immersed in the moon itself. Just as a lamp gives light without losing its power as a lamp, the moon reflects the light of the Sun without losing its power to do so.

Contemplation 57

The beauty of a pearl is perceived through its radiance. So too, the beauty of Shiva is perceived through the radiance of the Shakti.

Contemplation 58

The Mantra Om is made up of the three letters A,U,M. Does the fact that these are three separate letters mean that Om is separate from God?

Contemplation 59

Water enjoys the fragrance of flower buds by its ripples that smell the buds. Yet, the water is unchanged by its rippling and the fragrance it inherits from the flower buds.

Contemplation 60

Therefore, I bow to Shiva and Shakti without making any distinction between them.

Contemplation 61

When a mirror is set aside, the reflection of an object remains one with the object. When air is still, ripples dissolve in water.

Contemplation 62

When one awakes from the sleep of ignorance, one realizes that the Shiva-Shakti power alone exists, masquerading as all the objects of this world-appearance. To that Shiva-Shakti power I bow over and over again.

Contemplation 63

As salt poured into the ocean dissolves in the ocean and loses its separate identity as salt, in the same way, by surrendering my ego to that Shiva-Shakti power, my ego was destroyed and only that Shiva-Shakti remained.

Contemplation 64

In this way, I have glorified that Shiva-Shakti power by merging in it, allowing my false identity as the body, mind and senses to be erased.

Chapter 2
Praise for the Sadguru

Contemplation 1

To that One who waters and nurtures my endeavors in a
sacred bond of power and, although formless, has assumed
the form of mercy.

Contemplation 2

Who, out of great Love and Compassion rescues the Great
Lord who has taken the form of the individual bound souls
lost in the forest of ignorance.

Contemplation 3

Who destroys the illusion of Shiva's Maya and serves the
delicacy prepared from the wisdom and power of
Liberation, to that worthy Sadguru, Nivrittinatha, I bow.

Contemplation 4

Merely by the gracious glance of the Sadguru, the bondage
of ignorance is loosened and the great Lord who, parading
as the individual bound soul, has forgotten his true nature is
restored to his true state.

Contemplation 5

The Sadguru engages in the charitable giving of gold, in the
form of Liberation, and makes no distinction between high
and low, great or small. The Sadguru shows the seer what
should be seen.

Contemplation 6

The Sadguru's power is the greatness of God and is the mirror through which the Jiva (individual bound soul) experiences the indescribable Joy of the Self.

Contemplation 7

His transformative Grace gives rise to the full moon of spiritual knowledge.

Contemplation 8

Upon meeting the Sadguru, the seeking and struggle of the Disciple comes to an end, just as a rushing, frantic river finds peace and solace in reaching the ocean.

Contemplation 9

In his absence, the seer becomes the various objects of seeing in the disguise of duality and diversity. But the moment there is a bond of power with the Sadguru, duality and diversity cease to be.

Contemplation 10

Ignorance, that is like the darkness of night, vanishes by the light of Self-realization that dispels the darkness by the Grace of the Sadguru.

Contemplation 11

The individual bound soul is purified by the Blessing of the Guru's Grace and no longer permits himself to be contaminated by Shiva's Maya (the illusory aspect of worldliness).

Contemplation 12

The Sadguru protects the Disciple during the Disciple's spiritual evolution while reminding the Disciple that Guru and Disciple are One. This is the glory of the Sadguru.

Contemplation 13

God, not wanting to remain hidden from seekers of the Truth, plays the role of both Guru and Disciple.

Contemplation 14

By the Blessing of the Guru's Grace, ignorance is destroyed and the spiritual aspirant is inundated with the nectar of wisdom and the experience of the indescribable Joy of the Self.

Contemplation 15

By the Blessing of the Sadguru's Grace, one begins to understand and experience that the knower, the object to be known and the means of knowing are all one in the same.

Contemplation 16

By the Grace of the Sadguru and the self-effort of the devotee, the devotee becomes a Disciple and, eventually, becomes one with Shiva. Without the Guru's Grace, the Disciple attains nothing and remains ignorant of the Truth.

Contemplation 17

When the spiritual aspirant surrenders to the Guru's instruction and command, the sacrifice in the form of that devotee's effort at Sadhana (daily spiritual practice instructed by the Guru) bears fruit in the form of permanent spiritual transformation and Liberation.

Contemplation 18

If a person's desire for spiritual progress does not embody the wisdom of the Vedas as transmitted by the Guru's Grace, that person cannot attain Liberation.

Contemplation 19

The Guru's Grace pierces the ignorance that causes a person to believe that objects are separate from God and separate from each other. In this way, the follower of such a Guru experiences all objects being reabsorbed into the Self. The Guru thanks his own Guru for this Grace-bestowing power.

Contemplation 20

Such a Sadguru has Humility as his greatest asset. Even though he occupies the great seat of wisdom and Shakti power, he remains a perfected Disciple of his own Guru. The Disciple of such a Sadguru is very fortunate to have that ignorance destroyed that does not exist.

Contemplation 21

The Guru rescues those who are drowning in the ocean of samsara (worldliness imprisoned by karmas). Those who are rescued in this way cease to exist as merely the body, mind and senses and, instead, realize their true nature as the Self.

Contemplation 22

The Sadguru is the Guru-principle, the light of which causes even the sun and the moon to shine.

Contemplation 23

Even Shiva serves the living Sadguru who leads devotees and Disciples in making the journey to Liberation.

Contemplation 24

Even though the living Guru is embodied, one should make no mistake about the fact that the Sadguru is the highest expression of the Shiva-Shakti power in form, and not merely the physical body of the Guru.

Contemplation 25

The living Sadguru is both immanent and transcendental. Occupying a human form, the Guru is not limited by that form and is all-pervasive.

Contemplation 26

The Sadguru cannot be understood from the perspective of worldly inferences and definitions and is not a person. God is the Guru and the Guru is God.

Contemplation 27

He is indescribable in terms of mundane existence and words become silent in his presence. He does not tolerate duality.

Contemplation 28

The Sadguru cannot be defined in common worldly terms. Such a Guru is self-effulgent and not self-proclaiming.

Contemplation 29

In order to understand and experience who the Guru is one has to change the prescription of one's glasses.

Contemplation 30

Although praise of the Sadguru inculcates Bhakti on the part of the devotee, the Sadguru does not want your praise. He wants your heart.

Contemplation 31

In the indescribable Joy of the Shiva-Shakti power there is no attachment. Therefore, the Guru cannot be said to be detached when he is not attached to anything or anyone. However, the Guru does not discard the humility, reverence and longing inculcated in the devotee/disciple who refers to him as 'Guru' or 'Sadguru.'

Contemplation 32

When there is nothing to be abandoned, what is there for the Guru to abandon? Therefore, why should he abandon the reference 'Guru' or 'Sadguru?'

Contemplation 33

The sun has never seen darkness but is falsely accused of being the enemy of darkness.

Contemplation 34

By the Sun of the Guru's Will and Grace, the dross of worldliness is purified, that which is dull shines and what is said cannot happen, happens.

Contemplation 35

Oh, Guru! Whatever you show through the immanent aspect of existence known as Shiva's Maya, you merge into the transcendental, pure Supreme Principle. Your true identity cannot be understood by way of worldly, societal norms.

Contemplation 36

As there, so here. Oh Sadguru! You are there, here and everywhere. How can we understand you as just a form, just a body, mind and senses? Your true nature is beyond these mundane perceptions.

Contemplation 37

You, dearest Sadguru are Shiva! You appear to be just a normal person. But upon closer examination, one does not know your true disposition. You can appear one way or another, but you are definitely beyond all appearances.

Contemplation 38

You play various roles that appear to describe your nature. Then you render them meaningless in the experience of who you really are. You are pleased with playing at various roles that are all the tools by which you extend your Grace and Blessings.

Contemplation 39

By way of Supreme Love, you erase the Disciple's false identity and take up residence in him.

Contemplation 40

You are That which is all-pervasive - Omniscient, Omnipotent and Omnipresent. You can only be understood in this way.

Contemplation 41

Just as night cannot survive the light of the sun and salt does not remain salt but dissolves in water, ignorance vanishes by your Grace and Blessings.

Contemplation 42

Just as camphor is devoured in the flame of a fire, in the same way, in your presence, names and forms are devoured in the fire of your Love.

Contemplation 43

The distinction I make between the Guru and myself is imaginary. From the Guru's perspective, the Guru and the Disciple are One. In this way, when I bow to the Guru, I bow to my very own Self.

Contemplation 44

Just as the sun does not rise to praise itself, the Guru does not accept my gesture of bowing to elevate himself. I bow to the Guru to inculcate Bhakti and the Guru accepts my Love in this way.

Contemplation 45

We are so used to worshipping forms in one way or another. It's an old, ingrained habit. Therefore, God takes the form of the Sadguru so that our worship of God can be filled with Bhakti and Supreme Love, by way of worship of the Guru-principle fully manifest in the form of the Sadguru.

Contemplation 46

As one's Sadhana advances, the worship of the living Guru's form is converted into that of the formless Absolute.

Contemplation 47

Remembering and worshipping the form of the Guru causes the mind to dissolve in the formless Absolute. What remains is the indescribable Joy of the inner Self.

Contemplation 48

By worship of the living Sadguru, the knot of the heart is released and ignorance flees. Then the ego-idea cannot rise.

Contemplation 49

Then the worshipper loses all sense of individuality and is carried away to Joy by the Grace and Blessing of the Guru.

Contemplation 50

Therefore, worship of the Sadguru leads to the dissolution of all forms in the ocean of God's Love. This is the Blessing of the Guru's Grace, combined with the Blessing of the devotee's self-effort at following the Guru's instruction.

Contemplation 51

The combination of the Guru's Grace and the Disciple's Grace inherent in this self-effort is what keeps the flame of the spiritual journey home burning. Without Bhakti (Devotion/mad Love for God and the Guru), this is not possible.

Contemplation 52

Just as when camphor and fire come into contact, they are both consumed and cease to exist, the bond of power between the Guru and the Disciple causes the false identity of the Disciple to be consumed in the fire of direct knowledge of the Self. The Guru and Disciple disappear in the indescribable Joy of the Self.

Contemplation 53

The worshipper and the worshipped merge into each other and become One in the Bliss of the Self.

Contemplation 54

When I bow down to my Guru, the illusion of duality disappears in my Love for him.

Contemplation 55

What a friendship I have! The perceived duality of Guru and Disciple is swallowed up in the fire of the Guru's Love.

Contemplation 56

How is it that the Sadguru establishes the only perfect relationship, the bond of power between Guru and Disciple? Such Grace is extraordinary.

Contemplation 57

The Guru is like the great sky of Consciousness containing the Universe of all the worlds. Even in the imaginary existence of what appears to be a world, he remains one with the formless Absolute.

Contemplation 58

Just as the ocean welcomes anyone who wants to swim in it, whether the person be virtuous or evil, the Sadguru welcomes all as God.

Contemplation 59

Just as light and darkness are contained in the One God, knowledge of the Self and ignorance of it are both a play of the Shakti of that great Lord.

Contemplation 60

God has two aspects; the transcendental and the immanent.
The Sadguru also has these two aspects. In the company of
the Guru, it becomes evident that God's immanent aspect,
this world of forms, is a magnificent expression of the
transcendental, the formless Absolute.

Contemplation 61

Therefore, it is the Guru who takes the form of both Guru
and Disciple.

Contemplation 62

There is no difference between gold and gold ornaments.
The gold ornaments are nothing but gold. There is no
difference between the sun and its light. The light of the
sun is nothing other than the sun itself.

Contemplation 63

Or camphor and its fragrance are camphor only and sugar
and its sweetness are sugar only.

Contemplation 64

In the same way, the Sadguru abides joyously as both Guru
and Disciple.

Contemplation 65

The reflection of a face in the mirror is understood to be
merely a reflection, an illusion that is not real.

Contemplation 66

When the formless Absolute is not yet manifest, the One
God appears to be sleeping. When awakened by that

Lord's Shakti, God becomes both the awakener and the awakened.

Contemplation 67

Just as the awakener and the awakened are one in the same, the Guru and the Disciple are one. This is how the bond of power between Guru and Disciple should be imbibed.

Contemplation 68

If, without a mirror the eye could see itself then likewise, I would be able to describe the play of the Guru's Shakti as this world. In this way, the Guru-Disciple relationship is a phenomenon of Grace that is truly beyond description but is readily experienced.

Contemplation 69

The Sadguru, without disturbing Unity, fosters the intimate relationship between Guru and Disciple that appears to take place in the realm of duality.

Contemplation 70

Nivritti is the name of my Guru. As with all Siddha Gurus, abstention is his charisma. The Guru is the kingdom of God.

Contemplation 71

Although the Sadguru appears to act, he does nothing. It is the Guru-principle, God acting through the form of the Guru.

Contemplation 72

The Sadguru is not engaged in doership. Can one who delivers a gift on behalf of another claim to be the gift-giver?

Contemplation 73

The Guru is not like a fine piece of jewelry that is tucked into padding to enhance its luster. He is the Light of Consciousness, pure, effulgent and the Lord Paramount.

Contemplation 74

When the moon is nourished by reflecting the light of the sun it looks impressive by way of that light being attributed to it.

Contemplation 75

Similarly, the Sadguru becomes the object of enjoyment and that enjoyment is transformed into the Supreme Subject, the Self.

Contemplation 76

The Sadguru is the perfect mirror of God. The sight of such a Guru, when enjoyed, merges in the direct experience of the Bliss of the Absolute. Meditation on the form of the Sadguru is the easy means to lose oneself in the indescribable Joy of the Self.

Contemplation 77

When the darkness of night passes with the rising of the sun, is there any doubt that the darkness has been dispelled by the sun?

Contemplation 78

Therefore, the Sadguru is the destroyer of the darkness of ignorance. This can only be understood through direct experience born of the Guru's Grace and the devotee's Bhakti and self-effort. Then no other proof is required.

Contemplation 79

I bow at the feet of my Guru whose non-doership is Self-evolved.

Contemplation 80

By bowing at the feet of my Shri Gurudev, I am no longer bound by the four kinds of speech that I have surrendered to him.

Chapter 3
The Debt of Speech Per Se

Contemplation 1

The sleep of ignorance is due to the bondage of words.
These words are Mantras and some Mantras destroy the
contraction created by these words and other Mantras cause
that contraction.

Contemplation 2

The Mantras embodied in the four kinds of speech
(Vaikhari, Madhyama, Pashyanti, Para) dissolve in the
highest, Para, when speech is used to direct the mind to the
state of Liberation.

(Vaikhari – gross speech engaged with lips, tongue and
teeth, Madhyama – a subtler form of speech engaged in the
sound of a drum or other percussive instrument, Pashyanti
– an even subtler form of speech engaged in by way of the
sound created by string or wind instruments, Para – the
vibration of Divine Consciousness out of which the other
forms of speech manifest and in which they all dissolve.)

Contemplation 3

The body is impermanent and withers away, and when the
mind dissolves, the senses wither just as the rays of the sun
dissolve when the sun disappears.

Contemplation 4

When one awakes from sleep, the dreams of sleep die.
Likewise, when Vaikhari, Madhyama and Pashyanti merge
in Para, the death of ignorance dawns.

Contemplation 5

When iron is melted it lives in liquid form that then becomes fuel transformed into fire.

Contemplation 6

Salt dissolves in water but survives as the salty taste it creates in the water. The state of deep sleep manifests as the waking state when one's sleep ends.

Contemplation 7

Similarly, Vaikhari, Madhyama and Pashyanti, when sacrificed to Para, destroy ignorance and become the direct knowledge of the Self.

Contemplation 8

This sacrifice becomes the means to Self-realization.

Contemplation 9

The state of deep sleep (Sushupti) is very close to the state of Turiya (the state beyond the first three – as in Meditation). From deep sleep, one can enter the Turiya state by way of sustained awareness of the Self.

Contemplation 10

When ignorance thrives, it breeds the notion that a person is just the body, the mind and the senses. When ignorance is destroyed, direct knowledge of the Self, 'I am God,' is born.

Contemplation 11

The chains of the bondage of ignorance are released upon the dawning of Liberation.

Contemplation 12

Where there is no ignorance, there is no need for Liberation. 'Liberation' is an educational term to indicate the death of ignorance.

Contemplation 13

Just as goblins are imaginary, ignorance is also imaginary. It is a condition rendered by the false notion of being just the mind, the body and the senses.

Contemplation 14

Can a person who considers the destruction of a thing that does not exist, be called a wise person?

Contemplation 15

If bondage does not exist, what is there to be liberated from? However, the death of ignorance makes room for understanding what Liberation is.

Contemplation 16

The mundane knowledge used to carry out daily mundane existence is bondage to one who does not have direct knowledge and experience of the inner Self.

Contemplation 17

The play of the gunas and the malas keeps a person in a state of bondage.

Contemplation 18

This state of bondage is evident and can easily be observed in the experience of a restless mind.

Contemplation 19

Just as the sun is self-effulgent and shines independently of any other, direct knowledge of the Self, born of direct experience does not need the support of any other type of knowledge.

Contemplation 20

Just as a lamp would be useless if it required the help of another lamp, if Self-knowledge required the support of any other type of knowledge, it would not be Self-knowledge. It is Self-knowledge because it does not require the support of any other type of knowledge to understand and experience.

Contemplation 21

If you did not know that you are already with yourself, would you be able to find out by wandering from one country to another?

Contemplation 22

Because you know you are with yourself, that knowing is not something to seek praise about.

Contemplation 23

By your own power of concealment, you conceal your God nature from yourself. This is not a matter of losing something that must be found. It is a matter of forgetting who you really are.

Contemplation 24

Liberation destroys both ignorance and knowledge in the indescribable Joy of the inner Self.

Contemplation 25

When the ego-idea is surrendered to the Bliss of the Self, the desire for speech vanishes. Then the spontaneity of expression becomes the tool of speech that elucidates Supreme Love.

Contemplation 26

Ignorance is like firewood that becomes ashes when thrown into the fire. When ignorance is fed to the indescribable Joy of the Self, the ashes of ignorance give rise to Liberation.

Contemplation 27

Camphor merges in water by becoming fragrance. In the same way, ignorance merges in Shiva by becoming the Bliss of the Self.

Contemplation 28

When ash is smeared on the body, the particles of ash fall off but the color of the ash remains. Similarly, when the ashes of ignorance are perceived in Self, the particles of ignorance fall away to reveal the Bliss of the Absolute.

Contemplation 29

Just as water cannot be seen in a dried up stream but is still there as moisture, direct knowledge of God may appear to be fleeting at times, but remains evident in the form of the indescribable Joy of the inner Self.

Contemplation 30

This world-appearance is the shadow of Truth.

Contemplation 31

The direct experience of the Supreme swallows ignorance of the Self and forever abides in its natural, primordial state.

Contemplation 32

The debt of speech is a debt per se because it cannot be redeemed by abandoning speech. It is redeemed at the feet of the Sadguru only.

Contemplation 33

Therefore, Vaikhari, Madhyama and Pashyanti should be merged in Para. In this way, by the Grace of the Guru, the debt of speech is discharged. There is no other way to be freed from ignorance.

Chapter 4
The Destruction of
Ignorance by Knowledge

Contemplation 1

Just as sleep disappears in the waking state, ignorance
disappears by the dawning of direct knowledge of the inner
Self.

Contemplation 2

The reflection of God's immanent aspect as this world of
forms is the experience of Oneness with God when the
reflections are understood as expressions of God's
transcendental aspect.

Contemplation 3

The indescribable Joy of the Self secures the experience of
unity between God and this world-appearance. Since God
alone exists, in this way, knowledge of the highest non-
dualism is like a knife piercing itself.

Contemplation 4

The silkworm makes the cocoon that imprisons it and
exposes itself to the danger of being suffocated; just as a
thief binds himself hiding in the bundle of stolen items.

Contemplation 5

Or fire consumes itself in the process of burning camphor.
In the same way, knowledge dissolves in Bliss upon

destroying ignorance.

Contemplation 6

Without the existence of ignorance, knowledge destroys itself in the Bliss of the Absolute.

Contemplation 7

A burning wick becomes brighter just before burning out, indicating that its end is near.

Contemplation 8

Who can tell when the jasmine flower will bloom or wither? But the death of its form is certain.

Contemplation 9

Ripples in water die in union with water. The flash of a lightning bolt is also its death.

Contemplation 10

Similarly, when knowledge of the Self causes the death of ignorance, knowledge itself dissolves. Where there is no ignorance, can knowledge be said to exist?

Contemplation 11

At the time of the dissolution of the world, the deluge submerges land and water so completely, leaving no boundaries or limits between the two.

Contemplation 12

When the sun's orb expands beyond the known universe, darkness is merged into the light of the sun and only that light remains.

Contemplation 13

Deep sleep is destroyed in the rising of the waking state.

Contemplation 14

Similarly, when knowledge destroys ignorance by way of its expansion, ignorance and knowledge become the indescribable Joy of the inner Self.

Contemplation 15

When knowledge and ignorance merge in the indescribable Joy of the inner Self, both cease to exist.

Contemplation 16

God can be compared to the sun that is the most brilliant and never loses its brilliance even when darkness appears.

Contemplation 17

So, it is the same with direct knowledge of the Self that cannot be illumined by any other form of knowledge, nor darkened by ignorance.

Contemplation 18

Knowledge of the Self illumines the world but the world cannot illumine this pure knowledge.

Contemplation 19

Only pure knowledge can illumine pure knowledge just as God alone can illumine God.

Contemplation 20

This knowledge of the inner Self is known as knowledge per se.

Contemplation 21

This is so because ignorance is imaginary. It does not actually exist. Therefore, its counterpart, knowledge, cannot exist either.

Contemplation 22

Where there is no ignorance there is no knowledge either. There is just God abiding in God.

Contemplation 23

Of what use is light if there is no darkness?

Contemplation 24

So, the Supreme is beyond existence and non-existence, beyond all definitions, beyond all language and educational terms used to indicate it.

Contemplation 25

Can something that always has been and always will be suddenly come into existence? Even such existence is imaginary.

Contemplation 26

God alone is.

Contemplation 27

If the person who turns off a light then disappears, who will there be to tell if there was any light or not?

Contemplation 28

Or were a person to pass away in his sleep, who could then tell if he had a sound sleep or not?

Contemplation 29

Who can tell if a pot is broken or not, if there is no one to speak of it?

Contemplation 30

Therefore, Pure Knowledge, direct knowledge of the Self does not perceive it to be existent or non-existent. The Self is, without being existent or non-existent.

Contemplation 31

Duality and diversity exist only in name, in ignorance. Such notions dissolve upon the experience of Pure Knowledge.

Contemplation 32

But because knowledge of the Self cannot be perceived through the mind or the senses, can it be said that this knowledge does not exist?

Contemplation 33

So, the Pure Knowledge is knowledge per se.

Contemplation 34

When there is awareness of God as God, Pure Knowledge has become that awareness of the Absolute.

Contemplation 35

In this way, that knowledge does exist as complete awareness of the highest.

Contemplation 36

If the water in a well is crystal clear, the well may appear to be dry but it is nothing but water.

Contemplation 37

Even if the water in a well appears to have dried up, the water is still there in the form of moisture.

Contemplation 38

Similarly, the Supreme Self abides in its natural, free state of being where notions of existence and non-existence dissolve.

Contemplation 39

In the experience of the indescribable Joy of the Self there is no awareness of sleep or wakefulness.

Contemplation 40

When Pure Knowledge merges in the state of Liberation, there is not even enough room to say 'I am God.'

Contemplation 41

This is the state of Self-realization that is known as beyond the beyond.

Chapter 5
Existence, Knowledge and Bliss

Contemplation 1

The formless Absolute is a triad of Existence, Knowledge and Bliss. These three are qualities of the formless Absolute that is beyond the beyond. Therefore, they are indicators of what cannot be adequately described in words but can be experienced directly.

Contemplation 2

Just as the shine, hardness and color of gold constitute gold, and the sweetness and fluidity of milk is milk, Existence, Knowledge and Bliss constitutes the One God.

Contemplation 3

Just as white color, fragrance and soft texture are one in the same in camphor, Existence, Knowledge and Bliss are the One God.

Contemplation 4

Just as camphor is easily recognized by its fragrance, the Self is recognized and experienced by Existence, Knowledge and Bliss.

Contemplation 5

Just as the color, fragrance and texture of camphor are not separate from camphor, Existence, Knowledge and Bliss are one with the inner Self.

Contemplation 6

Sat, Chit and Ananda (Existence, Knowledge and Bliss), appear to be separate in name only. They are one in God.

Contemplation 7

Just as sweetness cannot be distinguished from sugar, Existence means Knowledge and Bliss, Knowledge means Existence and Bliss, and Bliss means Existence and Knowledge. They cannot be distinguished from each other.

Contemplation 8

The moon remains a perfect whole, even though it waxes and wanes through sixteen phases. In the same way, Existence, Knowledge and Bliss remain one in the same, even though they may be experienced in phases.

Contemplation 9

Just as rainwater may be counted in drops while falling, but is all one puddle of water when landing, Existence, Knowledge and Bliss are indistinguishable from each other in direct experience.

Contemplation 10

It is called Sat (existence) to exclude Asat (non-existence), and Chit (direct knowledge of the Self) so as not to be confused with ignorance of the Self.

Contemplation 11

When pleasure and pain are destroyed in the Bliss of the inner Self, they cease to exist. Only Bliss, the indescribable Joy of the Self, remains. Then, even the labels 'Bliss' and 'Joy' disappear.

Contemplation 12

In the same way, the labels 'Sat,' 'Chit,' 'Ananda' are extinguished upon the destruction of ignorance of the Supreme.

Contemplation 13

Therefore, the words 'Sat,' 'Chit,' 'Ananda' as applied to God are indicators, educational terms expressed to understand what is greater than and the opposite of the bondage of ignorance.

Contemplation 14

Can the material world that is made visible by the light of the sun illuminate the sun?

Contemplation 15

Similarly, can proof of the existence of God be determined through talk about God?

Contemplation 16

God, the inner Self, cannot be demonstrated by way of discussion, just as the taste of salt cannot be experienced by discussing its uses.

Contemplation 17

The Supreme, the inner Self is the cause and the effect – self-established and evident by the existence of all that is experienced in mundane life. Forms are the proof that God exists.

Contemplation 18

The knower, that which is to be known and the means of knowing are all one in the same.

Contemplation 19

Therefore, the words 'Sat,' 'Chit,' and 'Ananda' exist to implore us to use the methods to experience God, the Supreme, directly.

Contemplation 20

The three words gain publicity among pandits and pundits, but they dissolve upon contact with the Supreme.

Contemplation 21

Just as clouds disappear in the sky after the rain passes and streams cease to exist when they merge in the seas and paths end at their destination, the three words vanish in the Bliss of the Self.

Contemplation 22

Just as the flower of a fruit tree disappears after giving rise to the fruit and the fruit crumples when yielding juice and the juice disappears giving satisfaction to the one drinking it, 'Sat,' 'Chit,' and 'Ananda' take to silence after revealing one's God nature.

Contemplation 23

Just as the hand offering the oblation to the fire loses all significance when the oblation is complete and the melody ceases to be after giving delight to the listener, these three words dissolve in the experience of the Supreme.

Contemplation 24

Just as the use of a mirror is no longer necessary when the reflection is seen and the one waking another leaves after waking the person up, these three (Sat, Chit and Ananda) retire in the completion of their glorifying God.

Contemplation 25

The words 'Sat,' 'Chit' and 'Ananda' dissolve upon contact with the Supreme.

Contemplation 26

Just as one cannot know one's exact height by measuring one's shadow, the Supreme cannot be known by the words 'Sat,' 'Chit,' 'Ananda.' The Supreme is indescribable, and yet the Supreme can be experienced. And the experience renders the three words whole.

Contemplation 27

One attempting to measure one's height by one's shadow realizes the futility of such action.

Contemplation 28

In the same way, trying to measure ignorance that does not really exist, then how can one say that knowledge exists?

Contemplation 29

The state of the pure experience of the Self destroys ignorance of the Self. However, upon destroying impurity, the pure loses its distinction as pure in the absence of impurity.

Contemplation 30

In the pure experience of the Self there is neither purity or impurity. So, what is the point of calling Consciousness 'pure?' Consciousness is.

Contemplation 31

In the condition of the indescribable Joy of the Self, what is the use of judging Joy?

Contemplation 32

Therefore, all such distinctions and notions provided by language as to the Supreme become null and void in the direct knowledge and experience of the Supreme.

Contemplation 33

In fact, in order to become established in the indescribable Joy (Bliss) of the inner Self, all such distinctions, notions and judgments must be abandoned.

Contemplation 34

The experience of objects (people, places and things) involves an experiencer. That experiencer is the Supreme Self, the One God.

Contemplation 35

Happiness, in order to be happiness, cannot be dependent on anything or anyone outside yourself. For it is the Self, your God-nature alone that is happiness.

Contemplation 36

By Love for God, Grace enters you. However, God alone exists. This fact is revealed by Grace.

Contemplation 37

The Supreme Being is Joy.

Contemplation 38

The indescribable Joy of the Supreme Being, the Self is beyond both happiness and sorrow.

Contemplation 39

In order to experience the Self, your God-nature, all notions and intellectual theories must be discarded. Then the Supreme shines in its own glory and is immediately understood by way of direct experience.

Contemplation 40

The purified intellect alone knows the Bliss of the Self.

Contemplation 41

The Self of all alone knows the sound of an unstruck drum or harp.

Contemplation 42

The Supreme Being becomes the honey in a flower and then becomes the bee in order to taste the honey.

Contemplation 43

The greatness of the taste of food that is not yet cooked is known only to that One who has become the food.

Contemplation 44

In the same way, happiness is inherent in God alone, therefore only God enjoys that happiness that is one with his own nature – one with your true nature.

Contemplation 45

When the sun shines, the moon does not cease to exist. At that time, moonlight is known to the moon only.

Contemplation 46

Similarly, in the Supreme, beauty exists without form, there is youth in absence of a body and virtuous deeds are offered without the doership of action.

Contemplation 47

Just as the sensation of sexual intoxication rises before the mind manifests to focus on it, the unmanifest Supreme manifests out of the spark of its Shakti.

Contemplation 48

The music that is yet to manifest is known by that One who causes it to manifest.

Contemplation 49

Just as fire is inherent in wood, the Supreme exists in all forms and is the cause of their manifestation.

Contemplation 50

Only those who can experience beauty in their own face without a mirror can realize the secret of the self-evident Supreme.

Contemplation 51

It can be understood in the following way; the crop is fully manifest in the seed, even before it is sown.

Contemplation 52

So, the Supreme is neither common or uncommon and enjoys its existence without a second, as the expression of all the forms that it causes to manifest.

Contemplation 53

What else can be said? That One God is understood and experienced in complete silence of mind.

Contemplation 54

The Supreme cannot be proved by descriptions, anecdotes, illustrations or treatises. The proof of the Supreme is in knowledge, by way of direct experience when the mind has dissolved in the Bliss of the Self.

Contemplation 55

In fact, explanations of the Supreme cannot establish the Supreme. Just as intellectual discussions and presentations cannot identify That.

Contemplation 56

All effort to know the Self by way of speeches and discourses are rendered futile in the direct experience of the indescribable Joy of the Self.

Contemplation 57

When intellectual conclusions wrought by the restless mind are sacrificed to the Bliss of the Self, they die in the Joy of the Supreme.

Contemplation 58

Being forever handicapped by lack of experience, trying to know the Supreme by way of intellectual understanding is like committing suicide.

Contemplation 59

As talc is destroyed when all its layers are peeled away, the Self is exposed as the only experient when the restless mind is dissolved.

Contemplation 60

Just as the stalk of a plantain tree sheds its coverings in the heat, the individual identity is peeled back when exposed to the fire of the Supreme.

Contemplation 61

In the same way, when the object of experience is caused to merge in the experiencer, they both vanish in the indescribable Joy of the Self.

Contemplation 62

There are no words to adequately describe the Supreme. And yet, the direct experience speaks for itself.

Contemplation 63

In the experience of the indescribable Joy of the Self there is the death of words.

Contemplation 64

Just as after waking up there is no need to talk about waking up and, just as there is no need for eating food after hunger has been satisfied, the pursuit of happiness is dispelled in the Bliss of the Self.

Contemplation 65

Just as there is no need for a lamp once the sun has risen and there is no need to plough a field that is full with the harvest, seeking comes to an end in the indescribable Joy of the Self.

Contemplation 66

Both the notion of bondage and the pursuit of freedom come to an end in the direct experience of the Supreme. All that remains is the inspiration to glorify *That*.

Contemplation 67

If the experience of the Supreme is forgotten, it can easily be recaptured by remembrance of the Self by the methods taught by a Sadguru.

Contemplation 68

Although words are popular and can serve as a reminder of God, they have no virtue to boast of, separate from the glorification of the Absolute from whom they gain their power.

Chapter 6
Disproving The Word

Contemplation 1

Hail to Mantra, God expressed in the form of the word.
Mantra is the donor of remembrance of the Supreme that
gives the experience of the formless Absolute, making it
tangible.

Contemplation 2

Just as one's reflection is clearly seen in a mirror, God is
reflected clearly and made visible through Mantra.

Contemplation 3

All words are mantras infused with the Shiva-Shakti power.
The foundation of these words is the sound vibration
emanating from the Supreme that gives mantras the power
to illuminate the unmanifest family of Shiva and Shakti.

Contemplation 4

The non-existent Self gives birth to words that are mantras.
These mantras bear the fruit of the Universe of all the
worlds and are the means by which all things are measured.

Contemplation 5

There are mantras and the there are Mantras. Mantras
(words) can reveal the Truth or conceal it. In this way, they
can keep one in a prison of illusion or free one from that
very prison.

Contemplation 6

When mantras take the side of ignorance, they make what is imaginary appear to be real, while making the Self, the only Reality appear to be false.

Contemplation 7

Like an exorcist, the Mantras of the Supreme cause one possessed of ignorance to enter the state of pure Shiva Consciousness.

Contemplation 8

One who is imprisoned by the notion of being just the mind, just the body and the senses, is released by Mantra. Mantra that reveals God is God.

Contemplation 9

Worldly experience cannot elucidate the power of Mantra, no more than the sun can prevent night from progressing. Ignorance cannot break ignorance.

Contemplation 10

In this world-appearance, activity and the absence of activity can only be properly understood by the experience of Mantra that is the cause of all manifestation, sustenance and withdrawal of appearances.

Contemplation 11

Mantra delivers one to the experience of the Bliss of the Self and sacrifices itself in the fire of that Joy.

Contemplation 12

Mantra, though famous as a reminder of the experience of God, dissolves in the final state of Liberation.

Contemplation 13

Indeed, in full absorption in the Absolute, there is not even enough room to say, "I am God." Mantra silences itself in this state.

Contemplation 14

God, whether remembered of forgotten, whether visible or not, remains One without a second: Omniscient, Omnipotent and Omnipresent.

Contemplation 15

The Self, the One God never forgets itself. Because God never forgets God, God does not remember God either.

Contemplation 16

Just as one who is fully awake does not need the remembrance of being awake, similarly there is neither forgetfulness or remembrance in the Supreme.

Contemplation 17

The sun knows nothing of night. So, how can it know day? In the same way, there is no duality in God who abides without remembrance or forgetfulness.

Contemplation 18

Where there is neither remembrance or forgetfulness, of what need is there for one who remembers? In the experience of the indescribable Joy of the Self, words and one who speaks words gladly die.

Contemplation 19

Although Mantras can serve a useful purpose in taking one beyond the mind and beyond the senses, in the state that is beyond the mind and the senses, all thinking meets with its own death.

Contemplation 20

If ignorance does not exist, one who says that Mantra destroys ignorance and then God reveals himself can be labeled as having gone mad.

Contemplation 21

Can it really be said that the sun destroys night in order to make its appearance as day? In the same way, ignorance, which is imaginary, cannot be said to meet with its destruction at the hand of knowledge.

Contemplation 22

Is there any need to awaken someone who is already fully awake? And can one claim to have woken up one who is already fully awake?

Contemplation 23

Because ignorance is imaginary, can the death of that which is imaginary cause God to be real?

Contemplation 24

Just as a barren woman cannot give birth to a child, ignorance cannot give birth to God.

Contemplation 25

Ignorance is as imaginary as a rainbow that, if real, an archer could tie a string to it to make a bow.

Contemplation 26

Trying to prove ignorance real is like attempting to sip the water of a mirage.

Contemplation 27

Just as fire cannot consume the sky, ignorance cannot live up to its name.

Contemplation 28

Darkness disappears in contact with light. Then there is nothing for the light to extinguish.

Contemplation 29

Just as using a lamp to see the light of day is futile, attempting to prove ignorance by the existence of the word ignorance is a futile endeavor.

Contemplation 30

Ignorance is the shadow of Truth.

Contemplation 31

Even though a dream may appear to be real, once awake the one having dreamt knows the dream was false. In the same way, when knowledge of the Self arises through direct experience, one realizes that ignorance does not exist, not even in the state of ignorance.

Contemplation 32

Can clothes be stolen off of one who is naked? So too, ignorance cannot be found and possessed in the direct experience of the Supreme.

Contemplation 33

Were one to eat food that is imaginary, it would amount to total fasting. Such is the futility of attempting to exonerate ignorance by the word ignorance.

Contemplation 34

Just as it is completely dry where there is a mirage of water, the mirage of ignorance is proved false in the direct experience of the Supreme.

Contemplation 35

To say ignorance exists is like saying a painting of land, rice fields and lakes is alive. The painting is alive in your imagination only and, therefore, not real.

Contemplation 36

If it were possible to write letters on paper with a solution of darkness, preparing ink would be a wasted effort. So too, attempting to prove the existence of the Supreme by imaginary ignorance is futile.

Contemplation 37

The appearance of the sky as blue is not what it seems. The imaginary appearance of ignorance should be understood in the same way.

Contemplation 38

Ignorance does not exist in the way the name Avidya
(ignorance) indicates. It can be understood as lack of direct
experience of the Self only.

Contemplation 39

Due to its inability to adequately describe the Supreme, yet
knowing it through direct experience, ignorance has proved
its non-existence.

Contemplation 40

God alone exists. In the direct experience of this fact, there
is no such thing as ignorance. There is only the play of the
Shakti as this world.

Contemplation 41

Intellectual understanding cannot support a destruction of
ignorance by the inner Self. The Self is like the sun that
has no darkness in it to destroy before revealing itself.
Therefore, ignorance is imaginary and the term 'ignorance'
is disproved.

Contemplation 42

Ignorance hides its own non-existence from itself. But its
non-existence is proved by the direct experience of the One
God.

Contemplation 43

So, it has been shown that, in the experience that God alone
exists, ignorance is an empty word. Therefore, how can the
word ignorance prove the existence of ignorance?

Contemplation 44

One cannot strike a shadow with an iron bar nor slap the sky with one's hand. Attempting to prove the existence of ignorance in the body of Supreme Consciousness is just like this.

Contemplation 45

Can one drink a mirage of water or hug the sky, or kiss a reflection? So too, ignorance in the Supreme cannot be found.

Contemplation 46

In fact, it is merely wasted effort to attempt to destroy imaginary ignorance. There is nothing to the word ignorance that justifies such wasted effort.

Contemplation 47

Just as one cannot peel the sky, ignorance cannot be destroyed by ignorance.

Contemplation 48

Like trying to draw milk from the nipple of a male goat, attempting to verify the existence of ignorance in the Absolute is a non-starter.

Contemplation 49

Like trying to squeeze juice from a walnut, the effort to discover ignorance in the Self is futile.

Contemplation 50

Like trying to push a river upstream with the hands, or like trying to turn over a shadow, or like trying to twist the wind

into the form of a rope, searching for ignorance in the
Supreme is nonsense.

Contemplation 51

Like trying to kill a ghost seen in one's dream, or
attempting to stuff a pillow with the reflection of cotton, or
combing the hair on the back of one's hand, the pursuit of
ignorance by ignorance is ignorant.

Contemplation 52

Can a non-existent pot be broken? Can flowers be plucked
from the sky? Can horns be plucked from a hare when
hares have no horns? Can ignorance be found where it
does not exist?

Contemplation 53

Can ink be gotten from camphor? Can the child of a barren
woman marry another? Can the word ignorance describe
the absence of it?

Contemplation 54

Like trying to find moonlight on the new-moon day, or like
trying to find fish in a mirage of water, trying to find
ignorance in the Supreme is just like this.

Contemplation 55

How much can this be discussed? Ignorance does not exist
in the Self. So, how can it be destroyed by intellectual
understanding that becomes useless in the direct experience
of the Supreme?

Contemplation 56

The word 'ignorance' does not constitute evidence of ignorance in the Self by attempting to destroy that which does not exist, no more than it cannot be shown that darkness exists in darkness.

Contemplation 57

Ignorance is a play of the Shakti. From the awareness of the Supreme it has no form and proving its existence is like trying to light a courtyard with a lamp at noon when there are no clouds.

Contemplation 58

Attempting to justify the existence of ignorance in the Supreme is like trying to harvest crops from a field where no seed has been sown.

Contemplation 59

One who is naked cannot claim to be clothed. In the same way, ignorance is an empty word, naked in the Light of the inner Self.

Contemplation 60

Is there a need for rain where there is plenty of water? So, what is the need or use of the word 'ignorance' in the direct experience of the Supreme?

Contemplation 61

Just as the sky cannot be measured and a lamp that will not light is of no use in the dark, the word ignorance is useless to understand what the Self is.

Contemplation 62

Without the ability of the tongue to taste, tasting is merely a name, an empty word. In the same way, in the experience of the Supreme, there is no experience of ignorance. Of what use is the name 'ignorance' then?

Contemplation 63

If the marriage results in divorce, is there a husband or wife? Can the plantain be tasted by eating the root of the tree? In the same way, ignorance cannot reveal the Self and only attests to its falsehood.

Contemplation 64

Like the sun, the Supreme castes its Divine Light on all gross and subtle objects. Ignorance is useless to understand this.

Contemplation 65

Just as one cannot see sleep in the waking state, ignorance ceases to exist in one who is fully awake to the Self.

Contemplation 66

Searching for ignorance in the Supreme is like searching for the moon in broad daylight. The search for what does not exist is futile.

Contemplation 67

A blank page cannot be read. It is impossible to walk across the sky and ignorance is nowhere to be found in the Self.

Contemplation 68

Any attempt to destroy ignorance by reason is meaningless chatter. Ignorance becomes helpless in the experience of indescribable Joy. Then there is nothing further to be said about its existence.

Contemplation 69

Just as the light of the full moon does not destroy darkness, reason is incapable of destroying ignorance.

Contemplation 70

If one does not take food, one is fasting. A person with no eyesight is blind. And a person with no awareness of the Supreme is said to be suffering from ignorance.

Contemplation 71

And yet, the word ignorance cannot convey the meaning of that which does not exist. Therefore, ignorance can only be understood as lacking direct knowledge of the Truth, the inner Self.

Contemplation 72

So, can it really be said that ignorance does not exist? The word itself is useless in destroying ignorance. The word only has any meaning in the pursuit of the direct experience of the Supreme.

Contemplation 73

Therefore, reason, in an attempt to destroy ignorance, brings about its own destruction.

Contemplation 74

If ignorance were to die, that would prove the credibility of the word ignorance. But, due to its non-existence in the Self, the word ignorance will not permit that to happen.

Contemplation 76

Can a person marry himself? Can the solar eclipse eclipse itself? So, of what use is the word ignorance in understanding and experiencing the Supreme?

Contemplation 77

Does the sky rush to meet itself? Can the palm of a hand touch itself? In the same way, can ignorance know itself?

Contemplation 78

Does the sun cause itself to rise? Can a fruit give birth to another fruit? Does smell enjoy its own fragrance? So, can ignorance prove its own existence?

Contemplation 79

Can water be made to drink itself? Then how can the word ignorance explain itself?

Contemplation 80

Is there any day when the sun can see itself? So, how can ignorance identify itself by the word ignorance?

Contemplation 81

Can fire burn itself? Then, how can ignorance destroy itself?

Contemplation 82

Can a person see one's face without a mirror? So, how can ignorance be understood as existing or not by the word ignorance?

Contemplation 83

Can sight see itself? Can taste taste itself? Can a person already awake wake himself up? It has never happened. Neither has ignorance established itself in the Supreme.

Contemplation 84

How can it be that sandalwood paste applies the paste to itself? Can color paint itself? Can pearl know its own luster? So, how can ignorance know of its own existence or non-existence?

Contemplation 85

How can gold measure its own value? Can a lamp light its own light? Does liquid know what liquidity is? So, the word ignorance cannot explain itself.

Contemplation 86

Can the moon know of its own movements in the sky? What of ignorance? Who knows of it?

Contemplation 87

Direct knowledge of the Self only establishes the existence of knowledge.

Contemplation 88

Knowledge, that which is to be known and the means of knowing are all one in the same.

Contemplation 89

Knowledge cannot know itself as a separate object of
knowledge, no more than a mirror can see itself.

Contemplation 90

Can a knife pierce itself? So, how can ignorance define
itself?

Contemplation 91

The tip of the tongue can taste many flavors but it cannot
taste itself. The existence of ignorance is like this.

Contemplation 92

And yet, the tongue has not stopped its function of tasting.
In the same way, ignorance functions as a play of the
Shakti only.

Contemplation 93

The Self, the formless Absolute that is Sat Chit Ananda is
full in itself and self-effulgent without reliance on anything
or anyone else. The word ignorance cannot offer any new
understanding or experience to the Self.

Contemplation 94

The Supreme does not allow itself to be proved or
disproved. So, of what use is ignorance in establishing
acceptance or rejection of the Supreme that can neither be
accepted or rejected?

Contemplation 95

Therefore, the word ignorance and its appearance cannot make the Self attain the state of the Self. So, of what use is the word ignorance?

Contemplation 96

A lit lamp cannot shed any light on or expel darkness in broad daylight. Such is the uselessness of the word ignorance on both accounts.

Contemplation 97

From the direct experience of God, ignorance does not exist. Therefore, it cannot be destroyed. And God is self-evident, so what is there to establish by the word ignorance?

Contemplation 98

The word, not having established its own usefulness in knowing the Bliss of the Self, drowned in its own apparent ignorance.

Contemplation 99

Therefore, from the experience of the Supreme, the word ignorance has absolutely no meaning.

Contemplation 100

The existence of ignorance in the Supreme is just empty talk.

Contemplation 101

Though appearing to have some significance for the unenlightened, the word ignorance, along with its assumptions, has become meaningless in the direct experience of the Truth.

Contemplation 102

When intellectual understanding dies in the Bliss of the Self, then knowledge and ignorance are understood to be just words indicating that which is so much greater than words. The indescribable Joy of the inner Self exposes these words as being unreal.

Contemplation 103

Both the words knowledge and ignorance, along with the assumptions they create, dissolve upon contact with the Supreme.

Chapter 7
Ignorance Is Imaginary

Contemplation 1

Were it not for the instigation of knowledge no one would
have even heard of ignorance.

Contemplation 2

Due to the fact that there is no ignorance in the Supreme
and the Supreme is both the cause and the effect of
everything and everyone, ignorance has no origin and is a
hoax.

Contemplation 3

Just as a dream is nothing more than a dream and darkness
is nothing more than darkness, ignorance has nothing to
boast of except itself.

Contemplation 4

Can one ride a horse made of clay? Can one wear
ornaments seen in a statue? In the same way, there is no
stock in embracing the imaginary ignorance.

Contemplation 5

Ignorance has no power other than that given it by the
Supreme. It is a play of the Shakti only.

Contemplation 6

In the play of the Shakti as this world, ignorance

masquerades as knowledge and knowledge masquerades as ignorance. In this way, they are very much alike in that the direct experience of the Supreme renders them both imaginary.

Contemplation 7

If ignorance does not exist can knowledge exist? From the direct experience of the Absolute, ignorance is imaginary. Therefore, knowledge is imaginary also.

Contemplation 8

If there were any ignorance in God, that ignorance would render God ignorant. This is an impossibility.

Contemplation 9

Ignorance can only perceive ignorance. It cannot perceive God.

Contemplation 10

God alone perceives God. So, where is the ignorance?

Contemplation 11

Some say that ignorance exists in the Supreme. If this were true, one would be able to find ignorance in the Bliss of the Self. It is nowhere to be found in that Bliss.

Contemplation 12

If ignorance, due to its own state of ignorance cannot testify to its existence, how can it be anything other than imaginary?

Contemplation 13

Ignorance cannot make itself known by itself. All things are known only by the Shakti of the Supreme that causes all objects (people, places and things) to manifest. There is no ignorance in the Supreme. So, how can ignorance even be verified?

Contemplation 14

There is only one knower, one Universal Experient that is the Self. If the Self is fooled by ignorance, who else is there to take note of that ignorance?

Contemplation 15

If ignorance has no power to make itself known in the Supreme, then can it be called ignorance? It is a play of the Shakti only.

Contemplation 16

If the sun were to be swallowed by the clouds, how would the clouds be visible without the sun? Therefore, even the word ignorance is manifest only by the power of the Supreme that does not contain it.

Contemplation 17

The Self, God, is the only knower. Ignorance has no meaning if not recognized by the knower as ignorance. Therefore, ignorance is not real. It is a play of the Shakti only.

Contemplation 18

Since ignorance does not exist in the Supreme, it is not discernable by the Supreme. In this way, ignorance remains ignorant of itself.

Contemplation 19

Cataracts cause blindness in the eye. So, where there is full eyesight there can be no cataract. Similarly, where there is complete awareness of the Supreme, the inner Self, there can be no ignorance.

Contemplation 20

If a fire does not consume the fuel fed to it, the fuel is powerless to burn anything. Likewise, since the Self cannot be consumed by ignorance, ignorance has no power and must be imaginary.

Contemplation 21

In light there is no darkness. In the Supreme, there is no ignorance.

Contemplation 22

Just as sleep is understood as not being awake, ignorance is only understood as not being aware of the Self.

Contemplation 23

Because ignorance cannot alter or take away anything from God, it must be imaginary.

Contemplation 24

Therefore, to say that there is ignorance in the Supreme is illogical.

Contemplation 25

Ignorance lacks knowledge of anything, whereas the Self is the knower of all things, and is the cause and the effect of all things. Therefore, ignorance is a play of the Shakti of the Self.

Contemplation 26

Just as dreaming and wakefulness are not the same, and remembrance and forgetfulness are two different things, ignorance should not be confused with the Supreme.

Contemplation 27

Just as where there is cold there is no heat and where there is heat there is not cold, and where there is light there is no darkness; where there is full awareness of the One God, there is no ignorance to be found anywhere.

Contemplation 28

Just as day cancels out night, awareness of the inner Self destroys the imaginary ignorance.

Contemplation 29

Just as death destroys life, the Supreme destroys the imaginary ignorance.

Contemplation 30

Therefore, it cannot, in any way be said that ignorance resides in God.

Contemplation 31

If darkness becomes light when the sun shines, so too ignorance is transformed into awareness of the Self when the light of the Self dawns.

Contemplation 32

Just as wood is consumed by fire, ignorance is consumed in the direct knowledge and experience of the Self.

Contemplation 33

The stream becomes the river by merging in the river. In the same way, ignorance becomes direct knowledge and experience of the Supreme by merging in the indescribable Joy of the Self.

Contemplation 34

In this way, when ignorance comes into contact with the Self, it becomes one with the Self by meeting with its own death.

Contemplation 35

Ignorance, upon contact with the Supreme, does not survive. Therefore, its existence cannot be proved.

Contemplation 36

Just as salt loses its identity upon dissolving in water, ignorance dissolves in the Supreme and can no longer recognize itself.

Contemplation 37

In this way, when ignorance no longer recognizes itself, that is recognition of the Supreme.

Contemplation 38

Ignorance is imaginary and, therefore, an illusion. An illusion cannot be driven away. Therefore, there is no need to worry about ignorance when full awareness of the Self

dawns. Then the imaginary ignorance proves itself to be
imaginary. So, what is there to drive out of the Supreme?

Contemplation 39

Just as darkness is swallowed up by the light of the full
moon ignorance is swallowed up in the light of the inner
Self.

Contemplation 40

Therefore, the word ignorance is vain. Because it is
imaginary its nature cannot be grasped by reasoning.

Contemplation 41

What is the real nature of ignorance? Because it is
imaginary it cannot be comprehended by the intellect. It
can only be inferred by way of ignorance.

Contemplation 42

Because the senses are also imaginary, whatever is deduced
by the senses regarding ignorance is also imaginary.

Contemplation 43

Ignorance seeming to be real is the outgrowth of ignorance.
It is the play of the Shakti as this world that causes
ignorance to claim its identity as ignorance.

Contemplation 44

Ignorance is a product of the prolonged dream of
worldliness. When one wakes up from this prolonged
dream ignorance vanishes.

Contemplation 45

The Supreme, having manifested the Universe of all the worlds in which ignorance is perceived to be real, is not defective. What is defective is the lack of direct experience of the play of the Shakti as this world.

Contemplation 46

The perception of ignorance is not the proof of ignorance. It is only the proof that the perception is defective.

Contemplation 47

Ignorance is found in itself only. This does not establish the existence of ignorance. It is only the proof that lack of direct experience of the Supreme causes the belief that ignorance is real.

Contemplation 48

In ignorance there is imaginary ignorance only.

Contemplation 49

What appears in a dream is imaginary. Therefore, ignorance, appearing in the prolonged dream of worldly life must also be imaginary.

Contemplation 50

Just as sugar cannot taste itself and a lamp does not light itself, ignorance cannot justify itself as ignorance. Only the play of the Shakti exists.

Contemplation 51

Just as cause and effect are not separate from each other, the impact of ignorance is ignorance only.

Contemplation 52

Therefore, if ignorance does not exist, knowledge of it does not exist either.

Contemplation 53

Just as it cannot be proved that sky flowers exist, there is no proof that ignorance is real.

Contemplation 54

So, because ignorance cannot prove its existence and there is no sign of it in the Supreme, ignorance is false.

Contemplation 55

Therefore, because ignorance is incapable of proving its existence in the Supreme, either directly or indirectly by inference, it stands disproved.

Contemplation 56

Ignorance is incapable of proving anything. So, how can it be recognized as true?

Contemplation 57

Ignorance cannot make the Self experience ignorance.

Contemplation 58

In the purity of the Self, in the Bliss of God, ignorance is nowhere to be found. There is only the play of the Shakti as this world.

Contemplation 60

When the Supreme is nothing but indescribable Joy, where is ignorance to be found?

Contemplation 61

Just as there is no need to remove soot from a lamp that has never been lit and, just as there is no shade from a tree that has not yet been planted, there is no need to remove ignorance from the Supreme.

Contemplation 62

Just as a mirror cannot be cleaned before it is made and fragrance cannot be applied to the body of someone who has not been born, ignorance cannot be proved to exist in the body of the Self.

Contemplation 63

Just as cream cannot be separated from milk, ignorance cannot separate itself from the Self to even call itself ignorance.

Contemplation 64

In the Atman, there is not even enough room to say, 'I am God.' So, how can there be any room to recognize ignorance?

Contemplation 65

In fact, ignorance has never existed in the Supreme. So, what is the point of talk about it not existing now?

Contemplation 66

The Atman, the Self is devoid of being or non-being. So, in truth, ignorance is rendered imaginary in what is.

Contemplation 67

Just as the breaking of a pitcher (which does not exist) into a thousand pieces is imaginary, ignorance is also imaginary in that it does not exist in That, the Self, which is alone real. Therefore, what need is there to remove ignorance from the Supreme?

Contemplation 68

Can sleep go to sleep? Can darkness fall into a well of darkness? In the same way, ignorance is unheard of in the awareness of the Supreme.

Contemplation 69

Can the sky fall down? Is non-existence embarrassed at its non-existence? Similarly, ignorance cannot defend itself.

Contemplation 70

Can the dead be poisoned? Is there any necessity to gag one who cannot speak? Is there a need to erase words that have never been written? In the same way, because ignorance is imaginary, there is no need to prove or disprove its existence.

Contemplation 71

Therefore, ignorance that has merged in the Supreme is no longer ignorance and, having merged in the Self, ignorance cannot prove its existence before having merged.

Contemplation 72

How can a barren woman give birth to a child? Can a parched seed sprout? How can the sun be seen in the darkness of night when there is no moonlight? Similarly, the existence of ignorance in the Self that alone exists is false.

Contemplation 73

In fact, there is no way to even trace ignorance in the Atman. It is merely a vague reference in a prolonged dream.

Contemplation 74

When seeking ignorance in the Atman, ignorance is dissolved in it. Therefore, even seeking ignorance in the Supreme leads to the destruction of even a notion of ignorance.

Contemplation 75

Can a person attempt to seize sleep in the waking state? So too, in the wakeful state of the awareness of the Self, ignorance is nowhere to be found.

Contemplation 76

In experiencing the expansion of the indescribable Joy of the Self, what point is there in searching for ignorance there in the Self? That which cannot be found in the Bliss of the Self cannot reveal itself.

Contemplation 77

In no way can any notion of ignorance reveal the Self.

Contemplation 78

Indeed! The vision of the Supreme has never proved the
existence of ignorance in the Supreme. Furthermore, the
experience of the Atman has never revealed a separate
thing known as ignorance.

Contemplation 79

No evidence can be found of ignorance, not even in a
dream. Losing patience with itself in the ocean of God's
Love, ignorance loses itself.

Contemplation 80

Considering all this, is there any path to ignorance in the
Self? God alone exists. So, where can ignorance be
found?

Contemplation 81

Attempting to find ignorance in the Supreme would be like
erecting a hall with pillars made from the horns of a hare
and trying to light that hall with the rays of the new moon!
A hare has no horns, there is no moonlight in the new moon
and ignorance cannot be found in the Self.

Contemplation 82

Can the children of a barren woman be garlanded with
flowers picked from the sky?! So, where is the ignorance
in the Atman?

Contemplation 83

Should one be able to fill the sky with ghee, only then
could there even be a fancy about ignorance being real.

Contemplation 84

By every means, the Sages of steady wisdom have tried to investigate the existence of ignorance. But it does not exist. How long should the Siddhas keep saying this?!

Contemplation 85

Do not be inclined to utter the word ignorance even in a dream.

Contemplation 86

The Shakti of the Supreme wants its own world, separate from the Atman. Thus, this world-appearance comes into being. From the perspective of ignorance, this world-appearance is real.

Contemplation 87

However, it is the Self, the Supreme only masquerading as this expansive world of objects perceived as people, places and things.

Contemplation 88

The appearance of objects is the proof that God alone exists here, there and everywhere.

Contemplation 89

When one does not have this outlook, that God alone exists, and that it is God who expresses God as the objects of this world-appearance, ignorance dawns. There is no doubt that ignorance exists in this way.

Contemplation 90

Just as seeing double when there is only one means there is a disease of the eyesight, seeing ignorance where God alone exists is the disease of ignorance.

Contemplation 91

Trees accept water from the earth only, and they become lush and green as a result. In the same way, the non-existence of ignorance should be accepted by way of direct knowledge and experience of the Supreme only. It is only in this way that ignorance can be understood for what it really is.

Contemplation 92

Just as one must conclude that trees absorb water through their roots, one can conclude that ignorance appears to exist only in the appearance of a world.

Contemplation 93

When fast asleep, one does not know of the existence of sleep except by its inference due to dreaming while sleeping. Similarly, when absorbed in the Self, there is no experience of ignorance. But its existence appears to be confirmed upon losing awareness of the Supreme in the prolonged dream of this world-appearance.

Contemplation 94

Therefore, because the world-appearance is a play of the Shakti, an expression of the One God, it can happily be stated that ignorance does not exist.

Contemplation 95

Just as the light of the sun cannot create darkness and cannot be called darkness, knowledge of the Self and the play of the Shakti as this world cannot be called ignorance, for it is knowledge of the Truth.

Contemplation 96

Just as the brightness of the sun's rays eclipses moonlight, direct knowledge and experience of the Supreme eclipses any notion of ignorance.

Contemplation 97

Just as water cannot burn anything, it cannot be claimed that ignorance is the cause of the manifestation of this world-appearance.

Contemplation 98

Just as the phases of moonlight dissolve with the new moon, the notion of ignorance dissolves in the direct knowledge and experience of the Self.

Contemplation 99

Can poison give nectar? So, ignorance cannot give the indescribable Joy of the Self. And, once that Joy is experienced, ignorance is proved to be imaginary.

Contemplation 100

When the manifestation, sustenance and withdrawal of this world-appearance takes place by the will and power of God, where is the ignorance in that?

Contemplation 101

God alone exists. The One God is both the cause and the effect of everything in form. Therefore, ignorance is nowhere to be found.

Contemplation 102

You cannot add to or take anything from the Supreme. The expression of the Supreme as the objects of this world is the proof that God alone exists here.

Contemplation 103

God has two aspects, the transcendental and the immanent. The immanent aspect is an expression of the transcendental. In the transcendental aspect, the notions of existence and non-existence disappear.

Contemplation 104

The presence of the Self, the One God that is both the cause and the effect of all sentient and insentient forms appears to exist as those separate forms. However, all the forms are reflections of That, the Self.

Contemplation 105

It is by God's power, the Shakti that all notions, ideas, thoughts and expressions appear. Therefore, even the notion that God does not exist can manifest only by way of the Shakti of the Supreme.

Contemplation 106

The all-knowing one is that one who observes, who witnesses the states of waking, dreaming, deep sleep and the state beyond those three. This all-knowing one is attributeless. And yet, it is also the cause of the appearance of attributes.

Contemplation 107

In God's transcendental aspect there are no attributes to describe. And yet, the indescribable Joy of the Self can be experienced in That.

Contemplation 108

Objects cannot illuminate God. Only God can illuminate God.

Contemplation 109

The ego refers to itself as 'I' and makes every attempt to protect itself from the Supreme.

Contemplation 110

The restless mind and the individual intellect think they are all-knowing. They fancy everything but the Supreme and don't see the ignorance in this.

Contemplation 111

The raging senses cannot perceive God.

Contemplation 112

How can the mind and the intellect fully comprehend the Self that is content with devouring all notions, including the notion of its non-existence?

Contemplation 113

Just as taste cannot taste itself, the Self cannot be known as an object of the mind or the senses. To know the Self, one must go beyond the mind and the senses, beyond all objectivity. Only that witness to the mind and the senses can provide evidence of the Supreme.

Contemplation 114

Ignorance, in the form of innumerable objects and names, when coming into contact with the Supreme, immediately dissolves.

Contemplation 115

In the transcendental state of the Self, there is no desire to see or experience anything. There is the spontaneous welling up of Bliss only.

Contemplation 116

One cannot cheat the Supreme. Any attempt to prove that there is ignorance in the Supreme is a losing proposition.

Contemplation 117

Can one measure one's shadow in order to jump over it? In the same way, ignorance cannot be measured in the Self in order to prove that it exists.

Contemplation 118

God cannot be defined as this or that. The only way to know God is through the direct experience that is beyond definitions.

Contemplation 119

The Self is beyond words and, yet, *That* can be experienced directly. In *That*, the knower, the means of knowing and that which is to be known are all one in the same.

Contemplation 120

How can there be any ignorance in the Self by whose all-knowing Shakti power one's vision is purified and restored?

Contemplation 121

In God's transcendental state, God is not an object since objects do not really exist in Consciousness. God alone exists. Objects (people, places and things) are imaginary. What is seen is a play of the Shakti only.

Contemplation 122

In the Self, who would meet whom? All names and forms are devoured in the indescribable Joy of the Self.

Contemplation 123

Setting aside all notions, definitions, ideas and concepts, God has opened the floodgates for light to enter.

Contemplation 124

The Supreme is the substratum, the cause and the effect of all the innumerable forms. These forms are the play of the Supreme.

Contemplation 125

Having lost itself in itself, the Shakti of the Supreme, the energy substratum of everything and everyone, is not interested in its reflections in the form of everything and everyone.

Contemplation 126

God is the great actor. God becomes the stage, the props, the costumes, the lights, the sound, the curtains and the cast. This is the play of the Shakti as this world.

Contemplation 127

God assumes all the forms like putting on a costume. God discards one costume for another in the process of playing all the roles on the world stage.

Contemplation 128

In this way, the Supreme wears the ornaments of existence in every moment as the possessor of them.

Contemplation 129

God becomes the Universe of all the worlds for the enjoyment of the play of the Shakti.

Contemplation 130

The Self is Omniscient, Omnipotent and Omnipresent. This power is not found anywhere else.

Contemplation 131

By its Shakti, the Supreme becomes the faculty of seeing, as well as what is seen and knowledge masquerades as ignorance.

Contemplation 132

Out of Joy, God becomes the objects to be seen and known.

Contemplation 133

Just as the unity of one's face is not broken when reflected in a mirror, the reflection known as the activity of this world-appearance is one, unified in the Self.

Contemplation 134

Just as a horse's position of standing never changes, even when the horse sleeps, the unity of God-consciousness is unbroken by the activity of this world-appearance.

Contemplation 135

Just as ripples in the water are water only, the manifestation of objects (people, places and things) in pure Consciousness is that Consciousness only.

Contemplation 136

Just as flames are fire only, objects are the Self only. God alone exists.

Contemplation 137

The rays of the sun are the sun only. It is the same with all objects that manifest by God's power.

Contemplation 138

Just as nothing is taken away or added to the moon by its rays of light, nothing can be added to or taken away from pure Consciousness, the One God that manifests the objects of this world-appearance.

Contemplation 139

The petals of the lotus flower are not different from the flower. In the same way, objects manifesting by the Shakti power of the Self are not different from the Self.

Contemplation 140

The king Sahasrarjuna had a thousand hands. Can it be said that he was the thousand and first? The Supreme has millions of eyes, arms, faces, ears, mouths and limbs, etc. of which the Supreme is the possessor.

Contemplation 141

The clothing loom has a cluster of innumerable threads, therefore the loom is nothing but threads. In the same way, the Supreme contains innumerable progeny in the form of objects (people, places and things). They are all the Supreme only.

Contemplation 142

Just as no matter how many words are spoken, they are speech only, no matter how many manifestations of the Self exist they are all the Self only.

Contemplation 143

The vision of objects (people, places and things) in this world-appearance is the seeing of the Atman only.

Contemplation 144

Just as a lump of jaggery (raw sugar) that is divided for selling in the market is sugar only, the fantasmagorical existence of objects in this world-appearance are the Supreme alone.

Contemplation 145

In fact, there is no distinction between God and the objects God causes to manifest. It is all God only.

Contemplation 146

Although God becomes all of the diverse forms that appear to support duality, and these forms appear to be separate from each other, they are one in God. God's unity is never disturbed.

Contemplation 147

Just as colored garments and white garments are thread only, the manifestation of a world of multiplicity is God only. The Shakti of the Supreme threads through everything and everyone equally.

Contemplation 148

The Self sees all without eyes.

Contemplation 149

Just as the tree is inherent in the seed, the Self, the One God is inherent in all. That Self is both the cause and the effect of all that is sentient and insentient.

Contemplation 150

The Supreme manifests, sustains and withdraws the universe of all the worlds within its own being.

Contemplation 151

When God sees God only, the manifest world is withdrawn in God.

Contemplation 152

Just as the ocean is contained in itself and the female tortoise withdraws her limbs inside its shell, the Supreme withdraws the universe of all the worlds within itself.

Contemplation 153

The moonlight is dissolved in the new moon. In the same way, objects are withdrawn and dissolve in the Self.

Contemplation 154

So too, the One God, the Supreme manifests, sustains and withdraws all objects within its own being.

Contemplation 155

When the Supreme, withdraws the world in itself, there is nothing and no one. All that remains is the indescribable Joy of the Self.

Contemplation 156

God is both the seer and the seen, the object of what is to be seen and known, as well as the knower of all objects (people, places and things).

Contemplation 157

As to the Supreme, *That* is the knower, the object to be known and the means of knowing.

Contemplation 158

Nothing exists that is not Shiva, the Self of all.

Contemplation 159

God, the Self is the knower and possessor of all things
sentient and insentient.

Contemplation 160

God, the Supreme is the cause and the effect of both
existence and non-existence.

Contemplation 161

Just as the color white is inherent in camphor as part of its
nature, the manifest world of objects is inherent and abides
in Consciousness, the Self.

Contemplation 162

Therefore, the Supreme sees itself only.

Contemplation 163

When Pure Consciousness recognizes itself as an object
(this), the Universe of all the worlds comes into being.

Contemplation 164

By the conjoining of letters and syllables into words and
sentences, the Supreme shines forth as the universe of all
the worlds.

Contemplation 165

Therefore, it is God who meets God upon expressing this
world-appearance as the objects of this world.

Contemplation 166

Nothing exists that is not Shiva, the Supreme. Only That can illuminate That. The Supreme is self-luminous.

Contemplation 167

All activity is manifested by God, the only cause and the only experient. This is like sandalwood smelling its own scent or nectar filling itself with nectar, or sugar tasting its own sweetness.

Contemplation 168

It is like fire heating itself.

Contemplation 169

Or like a creeper preparing its own shelter with no effort whatsoever.

Contemplation 170

Just as sunlight shines forth providing light in the gloaming when the sun is no longer visible, the Supreme, filled with its own Shakti, vibrates eternally.

Contemplation 171

The Supreme observes its manifestation as the universe of all the worlds for no reason whatsoever. It is all a play of the Shakti.

Contemplation 172

Just as the moon shines without seeing that there is any difference between darkness and light, the Atman causes the manifestation, sustenance and withdrawal of the universe of all the worlds without making any distinction between these acts.

Contemplation 173

The manifestation, sustenance and withdrawal of this world-appearance occurs by God's Will.

Contemplation 174

Any perceived difference between the seer and the seen, between the Supreme and the objects that manifest in the body of the Supreme dissolves upon contact with the Supreme.

Contemplation 175

Even so, with the appearance of the manifestation, sustenance and withdrawal of objects in Consciousness (the body of the Supreme) nothing actually takes place. It is all a play of the Shakti.

Contemplation 176

In this way, the seer and what is seen dissolve in each other, leaving only the Bliss of the Absolute.

Contemplation 177

Objects appearing in Consciousness are not extinguished in the way fire is extinguished by water. They are imaginary from the start and dissolve in the realization that they are imaginary and that God alone exists.

Contemplation 178

Just as when 1 is subtracted from 1, what is left is zero, when the realization that nothing exists that is not God dawns, the notion of objects as being separate from God is erased.

Contemplation 179

When one sees one's own reflection, upon realizing it is just a reflection, the notion of the reflection being real vanishes. In the same way, upon realizing that nothing exists that is not Shiva, all notions of separation between God and the objects reflected in God Consciousness vanish.

Contemplation 180

In fact, all notions of separation vanish in the experience of the indescribable Joy of the Self.

Contemplation 181

Whether in different locations or not, seas are water only. In the same way, although objects appear to be separate and diverse, they are all the Atman only.

Contemplation 182

In every moment of existence the knower, that which is to be known and the means of knowing are always one in the same. It is the Supreme that enjoys the manifest world as its own expression.

Contemplation 183

God has two aspects, the transcendental (formless) aspect and the immanent aspect (all that is in form). When God turns attention to seeing, the world of forms is born. When God withdraws the seeing faculty, turning it within, the world of forms is withdrawn back into the formless Absolute.

Contemplation 184

As soon as God's vision turns within, the manifest world disappears. Then, when the vision is extroverted, the world of forms comes into being. This is God's play.

Contemplation 185

Upon rising above the state of the seer and the object that is seen, there remains only the pure perceiving awareness of the Supreme.

Contemplation 186

In water, there is a perfect calm at the point that one ripple dissolves, before the next ripple forms. Similarly, at the point that an object in the mind dissolves, before another forms, there is perfect peace.

Contemplation 187

Just as there is a space between the end of sleep and being fully awake, there is a space between the breaths, a slight pause after inhalation and another after exhalation. When the mind merges in these spaces, there is peace.

Contemplation 188

When the mind is allowed to dissolve in the space between the breaths, the Atman is easily recognized and experienced.

Contemplation 189

The gloaming depicts this state beautifully at the moment the day has just ended and night has not yet been ushered in.

Contemplation 190

In the space between the breaths, when the Prana (life force) is merged in the Vibration of Divine Consciousness, the Bliss of the Supreme is experienced.

Contemplation 191

This experience can be likened to what would happen if all the senses were to enjoy their sense-objects simultaneously. Then the mind would be canceled.

Contemplation 192

When the object of sense perception and the one perceiving both disappear all that is left is the direct experience of the Atman.

Contemplation 193

Can a mirror claim to see or not see its own reflection in itself!? When the restless mind dissolves in the witnessing awareness that is beyond the mind and beyond the senses, all reflections in Consciousness dissolve.

Contemplation 194

Objects are reflected in Consciousness just as one's face is reflected in a mirror. Without the mirror or some reflecting surface, one cannot see one's own face. Without the Shakti of the Supreme, objects are not reflected in Consciousness.

Contemplation 195

Just as the sun is not aware of the purpose of its rising and setting, and yet casts its light in all directions, the Shakti of the Supreme manifests multitudinous forms for no specific purpose, and out of sheer Love and Joy.

Contemplation 196

Just as juice cannot drink itself, objects cannot appear on
their own. The appearance of objects occurs by the will
and play of the Shakti. Objects have no agency of their
own.

Contemplation 197

The Atman is self-luminous. It relies on nothing and no
one else to manifest, sustain and withdraw the universe of
all the worlds. Nothing can be added to the Atman and
nothing can be taken from it.

Contemplation 198

Although it appears that activity is diverse and duality is
real, nothing actually takes place. This is the nature of the
Supreme.

Contemplation 199

And yet, the Self goes on manifesting this world-
appearance that cannot be said to be real or unreal. It is all
just the play of the Shakti as this world.

Contemplation 200

The formless Absolute and the world of forms appear to
exist happily as equals but, when God alone exists, what is
there to compare to whom?

Contemplation 201

Both the world of forms and the formless disappear in the
direct knowledge and experience of the Self. In that
experience there is not even enough room to say, "I am
God." "This is the world." "That is God."

Contemplation 202

The seer and the seen are one in the same.

Contemplation 203

Objects manifest in Consciousness by the will of God, the Universal Experient.

Contemplation 204

Objects are not seen by God. God sees God only, whether objects are manifest or not.

Contemplation 205

Seeing a face in a mirror is a reflection only. The reflection of the Supreme as objects (people, places and things) is just like this. All are reflections of the Self.

Contemplation 206

When the seeing faculty merges in the Atman, it dissolves along with all that is seen.

Contemplation 207

Just as one dreaming of running while asleep is not really running, objects appearing in Consciousness are imaginary. Waking up from the illusion of worldliness brings the awareness of this fact.

Contemplation 208

If, while dreaming, one sees a headless couple sitting on the thrown of a kingdom, is that real or imaginary? So, in the same way, objects in this world-appearance are also imaginary. It is all a prolonged dream that you must wake up from.

Contemplation 209

What is the waking state is but a dream. Objects appear in Consciousness. There is no outer world and God alone exists.

Contemplation 210

A thirsty person looking for water in a desert cannot quench his thirst from a mirage. Looking for water where it is not is futile.

Contemplation 211

Can you take a shadow as your companion?

Contemplation 212

Therefore, what is seen and experienced in this world-appearance is the seer only. Objects are expressions of the One God.

Contemplation 213

God alone exists. The knower (seer), that which is to be known (seen) and the means of knowing (seeing) are all one in the same.

Contemplation 214

You can't see your own face without a mirror, but does that mean that your face is not there? Even without a mirror it is in itself.

Contemplation 215

Therefore, this world-appearance is a play of the Shakti, the illusory aspect of forms that are the expressions of the One Universal Experient.

Contemplation 216

The Atman is not an object of seeing. The Atman is That which manifests, sustains, withdraws, conceals and reveals that which is seen and experienced.

Contemplation 217

The proof of the existence of God is evident in the manifestation of the objects of this world-appearance. There is nothing else to be proved.

Contemplation 218

A coiled rope that appears to be like a serpent is rope only. In the same way, the multitudinous forms of this world-appearance are God alone.

Contemplation 219

The fact that a face is reflected in a mirror does not mean that the face is in the mirror. The face is in its own place.

Contemplation 220

In the same way, objects reflected in Consciousness are imaginary. Only the seer of those objects, the One God, is real.

Contemplation 221

Because they appear in Consciousness, even though objects are imaginary, they still exist as the Shakti of the Supreme.

Contemplation 222

The seer, the knower of the object is the Self.

Contemplation 223

There are no objects without God. In fact, because objects are imaginary, God sees God only.

Contemplation 224

Even if a mirror does not reflect a face, the face is still there in its own place.

Contemplation 225

In the same way, when objects are reflected in Consciousness and when they are no longer being reflected in Consciousness the Supreme remains and is unchanged.

Contemplation 226

Whether awake or asleep, a person still exists in form as the body. In the same way, whether manifesting, sustaining or withdrawing objects in Consciousness God is and remains unchanged.

Contemplation 227

Just as a king does not need to be reminded of his status as the king, the Supreme is not defined by the objects it causes to manifest.

Contemplation 228

The power of the Self is never diminished when the Self causes objects to manifest, to be sustained and then to be withdrawn.

Contemplation 229

There is nothing that can be added to the Supreme and nothing that can be taken away from That.

Contemplation 230

When the Atman decides to see, the world-appearance is born. When the Atman decides there is nothing to see, the world-appearance is withdrawn.

Contemplation 231

The Atman, the Supreme is both the cause, as well as the effect. This is a play of the Shakti.

Contemplation 232

Just as flames are nothing but fire, objects manifesting in Consciousness are nothing but God.

Contemplation 233

The Atman is both the seer and that which is seen.

Contemplation 234

The Supreme is self-luminous. All objects that manifest in Consciousness are illuminated by the Supreme.

Contemplation 235

What is visible is the expansion of the Self, by the play of its Shakti.

Contemplation 236

Ornaments made of gold are gold only.

Contemplation 237

Ripples of water are water only.

Contemplation 238

The fragrance in camphor is camphor only.

Contemplation 239

In the same way, objects manifesting in Consciousness are Consciousness only.

Contemplation 240

When you see an object, the seer of the object and the object itself are one in the same. God alone exists.

Contemplation 241

From the perspective of water, rivers and oceans are the same. They are water only.

Contemplation 242

Whether ghee is still hard or melted in a hot pan it is still ghee.

Contemplation 243

Flames, whether large or small are fire only.

Contemplation 244

In the same way, seeing and the object of seeing are one in the same. They are the vibration of the Atman only.

Contemplation 245

From the understanding and direct experience of the highest, it is God alone that vibrates. Nothing else exists. Therefore, what else is there to be seen?

Contemplation 246

Objects that are experienced in Consciousness are the
vibrations of the Atman only, the play of the Shakti of the
Supreme.

Contemplation 247

Just as ripples roll on water, gold covers itself with gold
and sight merges in what is seen, the Self sees and
experiences the Self only.

Contemplation 248

The appearance of the Self as the objects of this world is
like sound uniting with sound, fragrance meeting fragrance
and contentment realizing contentment.

Contemplation 249

The expression of the objects of this world is like sugar
covering itself and fire wrapping itself in flames.

Contemplation 250

The existence of the Supreme as the objects of this world is
like the sky expressing itself. What more can be said?

Contemplation 251

So too, the seeing of objects by the Atman is like seeing
nothing and the Atman's not seeing objects is like seeing
only that which exists.

Contemplation 252

In the direct experience of God words dissolve, knowledge
is knowledge per se and the boasting of experience is not
tolerated.

Contemplation 253

The seeing of objects by the Supreme is like this; nothing is seen but the Supreme.

Contemplation 254

The Self is illumined by the power of the Self and is fully awake without being awakened.

Contemplation 255

While becoming the multitudinous forms of the universe of all the worlds, the state of the Supreme is never disturbed and remains unchanged.

Contemplation 256

While reflecting all the forms in the mirror of its own Consciousness, the Self sees and does nothing. It remains as it is.

Contemplation 257

When God appears to expand it is all God. When God appears to contract it is still all God.

Contemplation 258

Just as the Sun knows nothing of light and darkness, God knows God only, even when manifesting diverse forms.

Contemplation 259

In the way that the Sun glows without any knowledge of darkness or light, God shines forth as the manifestation of all the forms without making any distinction between them.

Contemplation 260

God is the great actor, playing all the roles for his own sport.

Contemplation 261

Just as the ocean remains the ocean, no matter how many waves rise and fall in it, in the same way, the Supreme remains the Supreme, no matter how many forms are manifested, sustained and withdrawn in it.

Contemplation 262

All that manifests does so within the body of Supreme Consciousness, the Self. There is no outer world.

Contemplation 263

To get cloth, cotton must be split. But, to manifest an object in Consciousness requires only the will of God. That is effortless.

Contemplation 264

In order for ornaments to be made from gold the gold has to be broken down and processed. But, to sustain and withdraw objects in Consciousness nothing has to take place. God's will reigns supreme.

Contemplation 265

Air cannot move in any direction without the force of the wind. However, the Atman moves in all directions simultaneously and in an instant, without need of any support or mechanism with which to do so.

Contemplation 266

Therefore, there is nothing in this world-appearance borne of ideation that can be compared to the Atman. There is no comparison to the Atman.

Contemplation 267

The Supreme is full of Light and Love and is never empty in any way.

Contemplation 268

Thus God is the sovereign of everything and everyone, everywhere. There is nothing higher than God who enjoys his play of the Shakti without any break.

Contemplation 269

Whether you call the manifestation of this world-appearance ignorance or not, it is all a play of the Shakti.

Contemplation 270

God alone exists everywhere and in everything. Can that be called ignorance?

Contemplation 271

Therefore, since God alone exists, ignorance does not exist since there is no ignorance anywhere in God.

Contemplation 272

All objects (people, places and things) are illumined by God.

Contemplation 273

On account of the existence of the Atman all sentient and insentient beings exist.

Contemplation 274

Just as darkness cannot cover the sun, ignorance cannot be found in the Supreme.

Contemplation 275

Because there is no ignorance in the Supreme, knowledge cannot be found there either. It is merely knowledge per se. This is the play of the Shakti.

Contemplation 276

Just as fire cannot be contained in a wooden box, the Self cannot be limited by the material world.

Contemplation 277

God pulsates as the universe of all the worlds. Thinking and speech cannot touch God. But God can be realized and experienced by going beyond the mind and beyond the senses.

Contemplation 278

Direct knowledge of the Self, borne of direct experience destroys all doctrines of ignorance.

Contemplation 279

In the Bliss of the Absolute, ignorance has no meaning.

Contemplation 280

The Atman is the one, universal experient and sees itself
only by its own light.

Contemplation 281

Objects are called into the mind by their names, their
labels. Therefore, don't label it. Then all that is left is the
play of the Shakti as this world.

Contemplation 282

Ignorance exists in name only, conjured up in the mind by
its name. In this way, the imaginary ignorance appears to
be real.

Contemplation 283

Ignorance is merely an appearance of ignorance that
dissolves when its name is withdrawn from the mind and
offered to the Bliss of the Self.

Contemplation 284

Just as water cannot create pearls and ashes cannot keep a
lamp burning, the notion of ignorance requires direct
knowledge and experience of the Self to fully understand.

Contemplation 285

Ignorance cannot manifest knowledge no more than the sky
can drop down stone slabs.

Contemplation 286

Just as nectar does not contain poison, there is no ignorance
in the Supreme.

Contemplation 287

When ignorance comes into contact with direct knowledge and experience of the Self it ceases to be called ignorance.

Contemplation 288

Just as the sun is the sun only, the moon is the moon only and a lamp can only be compared to a lamp, the manifestation of objects in Consciousness is Consciousness only.

Contemplation 289

Where there is light there can be no darkness. In the same way, that which is illumined by the Atman is the Atman only.

Contemplation 290

This world-appearance can be perceived by God alone. So, who else exists but the perceiver?

Contemplation 291

The Atman is self-illumined by the Grace of the Atman that it takes great delight in.

Contemplation 292

Ignorance cannot give God the power to illuminate, as it is God who causes the notion of ignorance to manifest.

Contemplation 293

From the viewpoint of the Self, ignorance is unreal.

Contemplation 294

Just as the sun cannot collect darkness, even if attempting to do so, the Self cannot collect ignorance.

Contemplation 295

In the same way that, in wakefulness, sleep cannot be found, in the Supreme, ignorance cannot be found.

Chapter 8
Knowledge Per Se

Contemplation 1

You are the Self. This knowledge and direct experience is illumined by the Guru. Therefore, not only is it true that ignorance does not exist in you, but knowledge of any ignorance does not exist in you either.

Contemplation 2

When we try to see how we are instead of who we are the Supreme is concealed.

Contemplation 3

By the Grace and Blessings of the Guru we are able to experience the indescribable Joy of the Self in a way that cannot be contained.

Contemplation 4

In the state of Liberation, there is nothing to add. In the highest awareness of the Self there is no flaw.

Contemplation 5

In order to realize the Self it is necessary to go beyond the mind and beyond the senses to that Witness of all. Only that can be called awareness, being illumined by the Light of God.

Contemplation 6

In the world of forms God is the only one to be seen.

Contemplation 7

Existence, Consciousness and Bliss are eternal. In the state of Liberation nothing is concealed. All is revealed as the One God. That alone is knowledge.

Contemplation 8

The state of Liberation conferred by the Grace and Blessings of the Sadguru is indescribable. Yet it can be experienced. That experience is knowledge.

Contemplation 9

In the direct experience of the highest Bliss the illusion of Maya is destroyed. In the final dawning of Liberation Maya cannot come to life again.

Contemplation 10

Where there is no ignorance, there is only knowledge per se. In truth, in the experience of the Self there is witnessing awareness only.

Contemplation 11

Just as the light of a lamp is unnecessary when the sun is blazing, there is no need of knowledge when the Light of the Self is experienced.

Contemplation 12

Therefore, where there is no ignorance, knowledge of ignorance vanishes. All that is left is the awareness of the Supreme.

Contemplation 13

'Knowledge' and 'ignorance' give rise to a spat of interpretations. But direct experience of the Supreme cannot be argued with. That experience is beyond both knowledge and ignorance.

Contemplation 14

God has two aspects, the transcendental (the formless Absolute) and the immanent (the appearance of the world of forms). Without the transcendental aspect the immanent aspect cannot exist. The formless Absolute is both the cause and the effect of this world appearance.

Contemplation 15

Just as one cannot see objects clearly in the dark without light, the world of forms cannot be known and experienced without the Light of God.

Contemplation 16

Ignorance cannot be known as such without knowledge of the Supreme by which everything is known.

Contemplation 17

In this way, knowledge replaces ignorance. But both ignorance and knowledge are canceled in the direct experience of the indescribable Joy of the Self.

Contemplation 18

The one who knows, knows not and the one who does not know knows. Ignorance is sacrificed to knowledge and knowledge is sacrificed to the Bliss of the Supreme. What else can be said of the two?

Contemplation 19

The sun of Consciousness rises in the sky of Pure Knowledge. All else is knowledge per se.

Chapter 9
The State of Liberation Defined

Contemplation 1

The act of smelling has turned into the nose. The act of hearing has sprouted ears and mirrors have become eyes. This is the play of the Shakti as this world.

Contemplation 2

Fans oscillate with their own breeze and the heads of flowers with a sweet aroma have given way to scents to be smelled. This is all a play of the Shakti.

Contemplation 3

Due to God's first act of manifestation the tongue has become that which can be drunk, the lotus has bloomed as the sun and singing birds have become the moon.

Contemplation 4

The play of the Shakti has caused flowers to become honeybees, young girls to become youths and sleepy ones to become their own beds.

Contemplation 5

Due to the act of manifestation of the Supreme sight has turned into charming objects and pure gold has turned into well-carved ornaments.

Contemplation 6

The charming play of the Shakti has caused mango
blossoms to become cuckoos and flavors to turn into
gourmets.

Contemplation 7

In this way, the objects of enjoyment and their enjoyers,
and the objects of seeing and their seers all dissolve into the
indivisible Supreme.

Contemplation 8

Just as the chrysanthemum flower gives birth to many
blossoms while remaining chrysanthemum, the Self gives
birth to multitudinous forms while remaining the Self.

Contemplation 9

It appears that the world is full of activity but nothing
actually takes place. It is Shakti's illusion, the play of
Maya.

Contemplation 10

At the mere thought of objects of sense, the senses rush to
experience those objects. That is a play of the Shakti.

Contemplation 11

However, upon contact with the Supreme, the senses lose
their identity and become mute.

Contemplation 12

Although you may buy a gold earring, a gold bracelet and a
gold ring, the three appearing to be separate objects, in
truth you have bought gold only.

Contemplation 13

In an attempt to catch ripples with your hand you are left with water only. In the same way, objects appearing in Consciousness are God only.

Contemplation 14

The senses cannot exist or function without power. That power belongs to the Supreme.

Contemplation 15

The senses have no power of their own. Whatever pulsates in numerous forms that can be perceived by the senses is God alone.

Contemplation 16

The ears do not hear, the eyes do not see, the lips and tongue do not taste, the hands do not feel, the nose does not smell. The experience had through these occurs elsewhere in Consciousness.

Contemplation 17

Contact with objects of sense is imaginary, like the reflection of an image in water.

Contemplation 18

Just as pieces of sugar cane are just sugar and the rays of moonlight are just the moon, objects appearing in Consciousness are nothing but the Supreme.

Contemplation 19

The moonlight is one with the moon and raindrops on the ocean are one with the ocean. In the same way, objects of sense are one with the Perceiver of those objects.

Contemplation 20

The faculty of speech may utter anything but the source of all speech, the Self, is never disturbed by such expression.

Contemplation 21

While it appears that this world-appearance is full of activity, nothing actually takes place. It is a play of the Shakti only.

Contemplation 22

For the Liberated sage, all appearances of forms are imaginary, an illusion of Maya.

Contemplation 23

Just as the sun can never find darkness due to its own light, due to being one with the Light of Consciousness, the Liberated sage only experiences God everywhere, in every thing and every one.

Contemplation 24

For a person in the waking state, there is no dream state. Likewise, in the state of Liberation there is no other. God alone exists.

Contemplation 25

In the state of Liberation there is no attachment and, therefore, no attraction or aversion to objects (people, places and things). There is only the play of the Shakti.

Contemplation 26

In the state of Liberation, whatever the senses yield merge in God and nothing actually takes place.

Contemplation 27

For the Liberated sage the senses do not have to be restrained and humanity is expressed freely in the constant delight of the inner Self.

Contemplation 28

In the state of Liberation activity is engaged with elated dispassion from the witness to the mind that is beyond the body, mind and the senses.

Contemplation 29

In the courtyard of duality, the Self, the Shakti of the Supreme, of its own accord, threads through everything. When this fact is realized and experienced from moment to moment, as duality and differences appear to widen, the inner experience of unity becomes stronger.

Contemplation 30

In the state of Liberation enjoyment of sense objects expands the indescribable Joy of the Self. By way of Devotion a Yogi merges in this Joy.

Contemplation 31

Even though a liberated sage appears to be engaged in
activity, for such a being nothing actually takes place.

Contemplation 32

For a Liberated sage there is nothing gained or lost,
whether he/she is engaged in activity or not.

Contemplation 33

In the state of Liberation there is remembrance of God
alone in the recognition of the play of the Shakti as this
world. All else is neither remembered or forgotten.

Contemplation 34

For one who follows the will of God, the will of the Guru
only, actions are unrestrained.

Contemplation 35

For the Liberated, the destination and the path dissolve and
the universe of all the worlds becomes a resort full of Joy.

Contemplation 36

In the state of Liberation, one becomes both God and
devotee. Such a being is not engaged in doership and
enjoys the world of forms like a royal person.

Contemplation 37

For the Liberated there is no temple that can contain the
Bliss of the Self. For such a being space dissolves and
there is only the experience of timelessness.

Contemplation 38

In the state of Liberation there is not even enough room to say, "I am God."

Contemplation 39

For the Liberated sage it is God alone who plays all the roles, manifesting as all the forms in this world-appearance.

Contemplation 40

In the universe of all the worlds, God takes the form of everything and everyone, including the materials of worship, all mantras and all spiritual practices and rituals.

Contemplation 41

In all worship it is God alone worshipping God by God's power.

Contemplation 42

Just as the branches of a tree, its leaves and its roots are all the tree, all the forms manifest by God's power and are God alone.

Contemplation 43

All the items of worship of the Self are manifested by the Self.

Contemplation 44

For the Liberated, whether speaking or silent, it is God alone who speaks or remains silent.

Contemplation 45

All images of worship exist to inculcate Bhakti (devotion) and Mumukshutva (the burning longing to be free) in the worshipper.

Contemplation 46

For the Liberated sage God's Light never fades and cannot be diminished in any way.

Contemplation 47

Liberated beings emanate the Light of God at all times.

Contemplation 48

Contained in fire is the spark that is intrinsic to fire. Within all Siddhas there is the Grace-bestowing power of God. Here, the intrinsic spark is that Siddhas can only give Grace.

Contemplation 49

A Liberated being is God. For such a being, the state of indescribable Joy never diminishes, whether engaged in worship or not. The Liberated state itself is worship.

Contemplation 50

For one who is Liberated nothing actually takes place. So, how can there be action or non-action? In this state, Devotion merges in the indescribable Joy of the Self and it is confirmed that God alone exists and all are that One God.

Contemplation 51

Therefore, the declarations made in the Vedas and the Upanishads pale in comparison to the state of Liberation in which the Bliss of the Self renders sacred texts mute.

Contemplation 52

For the Liberated all scriptural injunctions merge in silence. There is great Joy in this silence that is pregnant with the vibration of Divine Consciousness.

Contemplation 53

When a Liberated sage walks and talks, that is pilgrimage to Lord Shiva. If such a being were to intentionally embark on a pilgrimage to Shiva, his going would be like not going anywhere.

Contemplation 54

In the state of Liberation, walking, talking, sleeping, eating, etc. amount to the same immersion in the Bliss of the Self. This experience is filled with wonder and awe.

Contemplation 55

Whatever a Liberated being happens to see he has the vision of God only.

Contemplation 56

In the state of Liberation there is no separation between the Liberated sage and God.

Contemplation 57

This state is like a ball that moves on its own, pushes itself to gain momentum and then rebounds within itself. In that play everything takes place while nothing happens at all.

Contemplation 58

In this way, the Play of the Shakti is the simple life of a Liberated being.

Contemplation 59

Drowned in Devotion, for the Liberated all activity is imaginary and knowledge of the Self eclipses knowledge itself.

Contemplation 60

For one who is Liberated, Devotion (Bhakti) is not created or destroyed. It is discovered as the natural, free state of one's being that has existed without beginning and without end. This alone is happiness that is not dependent on anything or anyone else.

Contemplation 61

Bhakti is the secret of all Yoga. Bhakti is also the secret to knowledge of the Supreme.

Contemplation 62

In the state of Liberation the various names for God dissolve in the direct experience of the Supreme.

Contemplation 63

For the Liberated sage Shiva and Shakti merge in an indescribable union filled with Joy.

Contemplation 64

Para, the formless Absolute, devours all forms and levels of speech. These are eclipsed by the Bliss of the Self.

Contemplation 65

Shiva is the vast land of Bliss without any boundaries. Shiva is both the cause and the effect that makes all that is manifest a dispenser of Joy.

Contemplation 66

The Supreme Self, Shiva, awakens those already awake, lulls to sleep those already asleep and causes those desirous of Liberation to realize the Self.

Contemplation 67

Whether knowing it or not, all belong to God and God belongs to all. God's Love is evident in the manifestation of the universe of all the worlds that springs from God's Joy alone. This truth is revealed by a Siddha Guru.

Contemplation 68

The Siddha Guru is the full embodiment of the formless Absolute. Such a being only takes our blindness from us while revealing what is already ours. In this way, the Siddha Guru is great beyond words.

Contemplation 69

The Siddha Guru is a great benefactor and savior. The qualities of such a being are known only to those who take refuge in him.

Contemplation 70

Living in a permanent state of equipoise, a Siddha Guru's
Grace and leadership are impeccable. Even the scriptures
and sacred texts of the Siddha lineage proclaim this.

Contemplation 71

You, the Sadguru (true Guru), the Siddha have become the
father, the mother and the entire family by destroying all
notions of 'I,' 'you,' 'mine' and 'thine.' When we
experience the indescribable Joy of the Self you are
mightily pleased.

More Books By This Author

VIBRATION OF DIVINE CONSCIOUSNESS
A Spiritual Autobiography
By Sadguru Kedarji

ISBN: 979-8-218-13365-8
The Bhakta School of Transformation, Inc.

THE VERSES ON WITNESS CONSCIOUSNESS
By Sadguru Kedarji

ISBN: 978-0-578-38070-4
The Bhakta School of Transformation, Inc.

THE ABODE OF GRACE
BHAGAWAN NITYANANDA OF GANESHPURI
By Sadguru Kedarji

ISBN: 979-8-218-18009-6
The Bhakta School of Transformation, Inc.

THE SUTRAS ON
THE 5-FOLD ACT OF DIVINE CONSCIOUSNESS
By Sadguru Kedarji

ISBN-979-8-218-19915-9
The Bhakta School of Transformation, Inc.

About
Nityananda Shaktipat Yoga

Love is the highest religion, the greatest spiritual path of humankind. Therefore, we welcome you with Love, we Honor you and we Respect you. In addition, our path of worship and study is led by Kedarji. He is a Sadguru (meaning true spiritual leader), holistic practitioner/researcher and natural healing scientist who has a reputation for leading without insisting that people follow. To this end, here you will experience programs that embody worship through meditation, chanting, prayer, contemplation and the study of scriptures/sacred texts. We are a non-denominational sanctuary of worship open to people of all paths and faiths.

For more information about programs, events, courses and retreats to strengthen the practices and awareness spoken of in this book visit

NityanandaShaktipatYoga.Org

RECOMMENDED FURTHER READING

The Verses On Witness Consciousness by Sadguru Kedarji
https://www.nityanandashaktipatyoga.org/books-on-meditation-the-verses-on-witness-consciousness/

Vibration of Divine Consciousness. A Spiritual Autobiography – by Sadguru Kedarji
https://www.nityanandashaktipatyoga.org/books-on-self-realization-vibration-of-divine-consciousness/

Websites

BhagawanNityananda.org
NityanandaShaktipatYoga.org
ShaktipatBlessing.org